Foreword
HAL LINDSEY

The Beautiful Side of

EVIL

Johanna Michaelsen

Harvest House Publishers
Eugene, Oregon 97402

Those names which, for any number of reasons, have been changed, are indicated by the use of an asterisk the first time they appear. All other names are the actual names of the persons mentioned, and permission has been obtained where deemed necessary.

Except where otherwise indicated, all scripture quotations are taken from the New American Standard Bible, © The Lockman Foundation 1960, 1962, 1963, 1968, 1971, 1972, 1973, 1975.

THE BEAUTIFUL SIDE OF EVIL

Copyright © 1982 Johanna Michaelsen
Published by Harvest House Publishers
Eugene, Oregon 97402
Library of Congress Catalog Card Number 82-082240
ISBN 0-89081-322-1

TO RANDOLPH
MY HUSBAND and FRIEND—
For his *agape* love

SPECIAL THANKS

—To Hal and Kim Lindsey—my family—for their love, constant encouragement, constructive input, and fervent prayers.

—To Dr. Os Guinness, Dr. Walter Martin, Brad Miner, H.G. Miller, John Odean, Mrs. Donna Odean, Ann Bare, and Elliot Miller for their thoughtful comments and insights. This would doubtless have been a better book had I more fully incorporated their suggestions. As it stands, however, responsibility for its contents is solely mine.

—To my mother, Paschal J. Abkarian, for many patient hours spent alternating between editing and comforting.

—To my father, Albert L. Abkarian, for his constant concern for my safety and well-being. Thanks, Tigerlily!

—To my cousin, Rose Marie Johnson, for her research work on Aunt Dixie.

—To Norma Van Deusen and Sondra Hirsch for their faithfulness in the tedious business of typing the manuscript.

—To the management and staff of Courtyard Cafe in Malaga Cove, California, for cheerfully accepting me as a semi-permanent fixture of their establishment for several weeks during the writing of this book.

—To the pastors and prayer warriors of the Vineyard Christian Fellowship of West Los Angeles, for their faithful intercession. God has used their prayers as a shield around me.

FOREWORD

The last fifteen years have witnessed an explosion of interest in psychic phenomena and parapsychology that is unprecedented in history. This fascination with things that are viewed as supernatural, or at least extra-natural, has permeated almost every level of society. This is especially true in the academic community, where only twenty years ago such interests would have been considered absurd.

But now, after almost two centuries of general skepticism toward the "miraculous," the secular world is being bombarded with growing evidence that there are indeed forces beyond the scope of the normal scientific process. Most major universities have added parapsychology departments that are not just studying the history, but exploring the mystery of the occult.

There is definite, validated evidence that unexplainable phenomena are taking place in various occultic practices. Medical doctors have verified many incidences of supernatural physical cures performed by psychic surgeons.

The question this book raises and truly answers is, Are these various psychic experiments and cures beneficial, or could they be an opening for enslavement to subtle spiritual beings of incredibly destructive intent?

Johanna Michaelsen is uniquely qualified to write about this subject. I have never met a person who has so sincerely and wholeheartedly explored this area. She studied with me at the Light and Power House school for several years. I have talked with her about her experiences at least eight years. When I first heard about them, I honestly wondered if they could be true. They were just so incredible it was overwhelming.

But since that time, I have had ample opportunity to verify the facts of her life fully. *I testify that this amazing story is absolutely true*. Johanna has become an expert in the psychic field and a gifted and powerful communicator about its implications to all who experiment with it.

This book is desperately needed when things predicted long ago by the Hebrew prophets are all being fulfilled before our eyes. The prophets particularly warned of a time when malevolent spirits would work amazingly deceptive miracles. I believe that we are witnessing the fulfillment of that prophecy on every side.

Words cannot express how strongly I recommend this book. I believe everyone should read it, whether or not they have been involved in occultic phenomena. I believe that *this book could literally save your life!*

—Hal Lindsey

CONTENTS

1
The Encounter

The tension was almost unbearable as we searched through the dark streets of Mexico City. We were lost. I peered at my watch in the light of a passing car. It was no use. Almost eight o'clock. We were too late to witness any of the operations scheduled for that night.

I felt a flash of anger as Tom stopped the car again to analyze his directions. It probably didn't matter that much to him or Norah*, his secretary, whether we arrived at Pachita's on time. They had both been there before to see her work. In fact, Tom* had an operation in which he claimed a rusty hunting knife had been plunged into his kneecap in order to repair an old football injury. No anesthesia or sophisticated antiseptic had been used. His knee was now fully healed.

As for myself, I knew I could come again another time to see the medium work. But Kim, my sister, was leaving Mexico the next day. This had been my last chance to make her understand.

"Well, there is nothing more I can do now," I thought. "It's in God's hands." I took a deep breath and forced my muscles to relax.

"This is it! We're here!" Tom exclaimed as he slammed on the brakes. He jerked the car into a parking space in front of an old market. The pungent-sweet odor of rotting garbage in the gutter stung my nostrils as I stepped out of the car. Even a lifetime in Mexico, born and bred, had not accustomed me to that smell.

We made our way across the dark street to a grimy white metal gate set into a long wall. The night was clear and still, yet as we stood there the sky suddenly filled with a host of unseen beings who swirled and spun around us with a sound like that of wind gusting through tall trees. My heart pounded in my throat. I was afraid. The others seemed oblivious to the motion all around them. I said nothing.

The metal gate swung open even as Tom knocked. We stepped into a narrow courtyard crowded with people, some obviously wealthy, others clothed in rags which spoke of abject poverty, but all drawn together by a common bond of suffering which reached out into the unknown for the ray of hope and healing denied them by conventional medicine.

A loud, angry voice broke through the hushed murmurings of the crowd. It belonged to a distinguished looking man with greying hair and mustache. He was dressed in black slacks and a white shirt with sleeves rolled up to his elbows. It was obvious from his manner that he held a position of authority. I backed out of the way into a corner by the gate as he waved a fist at Tom.

"There you are!" he shouted. "Come here. I want to talk to you!" His English was excellent, though heavily accented. "Do you know what happened here today? I will tell you. One of your Mind Control people showed up with motion picture cameras and demanded, *demanded* he be allowed to photograph Pachita during the operations. He said you sent him and refused to go when I told him this is not a circus act for curiosity seekers. He stuck a pin into Pachita to see whether she was in a trance and then tried to strike me when I ordered him out." His voice was shaking with anger.

"Dr. Carlos*, calm down!" Tom exclaimed. "I don't know anything about this. I didn't send him."

"I don't know whether you did or not—but I will tell you this: If you can't control your people and instill in them respect for the work that is done here, then not any of you will be welcome any longer in this place!" Dr. Carlos turned and disappeared into the crowd. Tom just shook his head and shrugged. After a few moments he followed in the direction the doctor had taken.

"Who was that?" I asked Norah, who had come up beside me.

"That," she said, "was Dr. Carlos. He's a surgeon—has his own practice in the area. He's been working as one of Pachita's main assistants for the last few months and is very protective of her. Come on. I'll take you in to meet her."

We made our way through the crowd, past an open sink filled with dirty dishes, then past a very ripe bathroom sheltered only by a flimsy plastic curtain. We were about to enter through a doorway when I heard a rustling sound above my head on the lintel. I looked straight up into a pair of beady little eyes that glinted at me over the top of a nasty looking beak.

"Oh, don't worry about *her*," Norah said a bit too softly. "That's Ursula, Pachita's pet falcon."

"How nice," I murmured to Ursula in what I hoped was an ingratiating fashion.

We stepped into the darkness of a small waiting room: empty but for an old metal desk and the sound of falcon talons digging into wood. The entrance to the operating room was shielded by another plastic curtain. Norah held it aside for me.

I was immediately overwhelmed by the smell in the room; musty dead roses and raw alcohol. The electric tingling I had felt upon crossing the threshold of Pachita's home now intensified, as though this room was the source of the current. The Lord's Prayer, which I had been quietly repeating over and over since we had arrived, was now screaming in my head. I stood in the doorway, unable to proceed, and looked around me.

The small room was lit by a single bulb which dangled from the ceiling. Eight or ten people, including Dr. Carlos, stood about talking quietly.

Against the bare cement wall on my right was a medicine cabinet. Past it, a rickety door opened onto the courtyard. To my left was a small wooden table cluttered with rolls of cotton and bottles of alcohol. The focal point, however, was a large, tiered altar which filled the left hand corner of the room. It was covered with dozens of jars and vases crowded with rotten roses.

A picture of Christ on the cross and a large wooden crucifix stood surrounded by white candles. Next to the crucifix, in the center of the altar, was a bronze statue of *Cuauhtemoc,* the Aztec prince who had defiantly borne torture and death at the hands of Spanish *conquistadores.* At its feet lay a pair of surgical scissors and a rusty hunting knife.

My eyes turned to the right side of the room. There, on a cot, sat a wide old woman. A worn blanket was wrapped about her legs. She was smoking a cigarette as she talked to Tom, who sat before her. I watched as her stubby hands made frequent though tired gestures to emphasize a word or phrase. They moved often through her short grey-black hair, then over her face, which she now rubbed as though exhausted.

I stepped forward and looked closer, unable at first to comprehend what I was seeing on those hands. They were covered to the wrist in dry, crusted blood.

Norah and Kim went forward to meet the old

woman. "Where is Johanna?" Tom asked, as he looked around. "Come on," he urged me, smiling. "Pachita, this is Johanna, one of my best students."

I approached and took her extended hand in my own as I looked down into a tired, very stern right eye. The left one was half closed as though from a mild stroke. I felt suddenly naked as her gaze focused on me. It was as sharp and piercing as that of the falcon on her lintel. Her gruff voice acknowledged my presence; then the eye turned again to Tom and I stepped back to the center of the room.

I turned to look again at the altar. Waves of soft light now seemed to be coming from the image of the warrior and the crucifix beside it. "Lord God," I whispered, "thank you for this place. After all the years of terror you have now brought me into a temple of light. Let me serve you here, Lord."

My prayer was interrupted by the voice of a sleek young man. "Tell me, what are you feeling?" he asked. With an effort I looked away from the glowing altar.

"I'm not sure," I answered softly. "I feel I'm in the presence of my God."

The young man nodded. "Then you must touch the statue of *Cuauhtemoc!*" he exclaimed. "Go, place your fingers on the statue three times!" There was a sense of urgency in his tone. "Go!"

I hesitated, afraid for a moment of the still shining statue.

"Our Father, who art in heaven..." I reached out my hand and with my fingertips lightly touched the image of the ancient Aztec warrior who was now Pachita's spirit guide, the one by whom the miracles of which I had heard spoken were performed. At the third touch a light shock ran through my fingers. My breath drew in sharply. I felt strangely light, detached. Even the Lord's

Prayer, which had been repeating over and over in my head almost of its own accord, grew still and silent. I was enveloped in a deep velvet peace which wrapped itself around me like a mantle on the shoulders of a priest.

The man took me by the hand and led me to the old woman on the cot. "Pachita, you must talk with this girl!" The tired face turned to me and focused on my eyes, staring through me with a frightening intensity. No word was spoken for many seconds. Then a blood-covered hand reached for one of mine and pulled me closer.

"You're very sensitive, very sensitive, aren't you?" she said softly. "Are you a medium?"

Her words startled me, and I hesitated.

"Well," she insisted, "are you a medium?"

"I...I'm not sure, Pachita," I answered. "Sometimes I think so."

"Well, my little one, you finish the studies in Mind Control you have begun with Tom and then return."

Then to herself she added, "We'll see. We'll see."

2
Great-Great Aunt Dixie

Aunt Dixie died soon after Mama was born. Dixie was Mama's grandfather's sister. Most of the family had been frightened of her and her strange powers. Yet there was a time when she was acclaimed by the crowned heads of Europe, including Victoria and the Prince of Wales. Her picture appeared in newspapers of Europe and America for over fifteen years.

Born Dixie Jarratt in Milledgeville, Georgia, she discovered her extraordinary gifts one night after attending a performance by Lula Hurst, one of the first so-called "electric wonder" girls who became quite the fashion in Georgia before the turn of the century. According to one newspaper article, the "Little Georgia Magnet's" performance lasted about two hours, during which she would, for example, place her hands upon a chair, and without clenching it, raise it from the floor. A dozen men were unable to put that chair on the floor or break her hold without twisting and jerking it. Nor were they able to lower a billiard cue held between her fingers or raise it from the floor when she placed it there.

She would lay her hands on a raised umbrella of steel frame, and the cover would suddenly rip off as though struck by lightning. In yet another test, she would, with one hand, raise a chair on which sat a large man, and hold it in her palm balanced on an egg. The article went on to say she had "many other tests and in no city where she appeared did anyone who witnessed her performances doubt the genuineness of her strange powers."[1]

Aunt Dixie was also known as a spiritualist and an effective trance medium. Often during a seance, faces of the dead would materialize on the wall and the entire house would shake and rattle as though in the grip of a giant terrier. She would awaken from her trance with a blinding headache and no memory of the events that had transpired. One ancient family member recollected that she could find lost articles and had tremendous strength while in a trance.

She died sometime in the 1920's, alone, forgotten and a pauper.

It wasn't until June of 1975, two years after it was all over, that I learned of her prediction: Someone in the third generation—*my* generation—was to inherit her talent.

---

[1] Source Unknown

3
The Intruder

"Are you sure you remember how to use this, Johanna?" I looked down at the loaded .32 automatic pistol in Papa's hand. "I think so, Daddy," I said, carefully taking the gun.

"All I do is pull back the top to cock it, aim, and then squeeze the trigger." I was only a few months away from my twelfth birthday and Papa felt it was time I learned how to use the weapons he kept in the house in case of an emergency.

Our colony was located on the outskirts of Cuernavaca—still at that time a charming old-fashioned town nestled in a green valley forty-five miles south of Mexico City. Papa had built our large, modern ranch-style home there six years before when the colony was just beginning. Many Americans and Europeans were building homes there now, but to get into town we still traveled twenty minutes on dirt roads that became treacherous bogs in the long rainy season. It would be another year before telephone lines reached us.

Papa's greatest concern, however, was the fact that a large settlement of squatters had recently taken over an enormous tract of land about a mile northeast of us. The land was owned by a group of Americans who had already begun paving roads and putting in electricity and water lines when the takeover occurred. The squatters were mostly fugitives from the neighboring state of Guerrero—murderers and thieves and refugees from clan wars who simply swarmed in with their families and took possession of the land under a provision of the 1910 Revolution: "The land belongs to the one who works it," and "Possession is nine points of the law."

Overnight their shanties sprang up and plowing sticks broke into land once set aside for more elegant homes. The police were hesitant about entering the squatters' settlement now since a number of patrolmen had been killed in ambush. Even the Mexican army had not been able to rout the outlaws.

The squatters left the foreigners below them pretty well alone, but on Saturday nights we could hear many of the men cavorting and singing through our streets, firing their guns in drunken abandon.

Papa had recently had a run-in with one of these outlaw *vaqueros*. The man had moved his cattle onto land that belonged to us. When Papa found out, he stuck a .45 in the belt of his white bermuda shorts and, in Spanish that was fractured almost beyond recognition even after fifteen years in Mexico, ordered the tall, handsome *vaquero* (who also carried a gun) to move "his filthy cows" off that land. The *vaquero* could have shot Papa dead before either had blinked twice. He had the reputation for it. But he saw the deadly gleam in Papa's eyes and evidently found himself respecting this brave but obviously crazy *gringo*. (Unbeknown to Papa, the *vaquero* had been teaching me how to milk those "filthy cows," and I was sorry to see them go.)

After this confrontation Papa took to firing his gun every week or so to remind everyone within hearing distance that he meant business and was not to be trifled with.

On this particular night, however, Papa was reminding me how to use a gun for a more specific reason. He and Mama were going out for the evening. Kim and I would be left alone in the house for the first time. We always had at least one live-in maid to care for us, but the latest one had been called home unexpectedly the day before and there had been no time to replace her.

"Are you sure you'll be all right?" Papa's face reflected his concern.

"We'll be fine, Daddy," I answered confidently.

"Well," he said smiling, "if anybody should break in, the sight of you waving that gun will probably scare him enough to send him screaming the other way. Come on. Let's make sure everything is locked up anyway."

I followed Papa into his room and watched as he locked the sliding door that led to the garden and pulled the curtains shut. He bolted the windows and then went into the suite Kim and I shared to make sure both doors and all windows were secured there as well. The ritual was repeated upstairs in the living room and servants' quarters.

"We won't be late, sweetheart," Mama said, kissing me good-bye. She looked so lovely in her soft cocktail dress.

"And you," she said to Kim, "off to bed now like a good girl. I am leaving Hungry outside to watch the house. You keep Houdini in with you, Johanna."

Hungry was pure mutt, an exact replica of Old Yeller, but Papa always insisted he was an Abyssinian mountain lion hunter, whatever that was. He thought it made poor Hungry sound ferocious and exotic, I suppose.

"Oh, don't worry about opening the gate. I've got the keys with me," Papa said as he kissed my forehead.

He then pulled the front door shut and locked it from the outside. I could hear him struggling to put the key on his keychain so as not to lose it as he had his other set months before. This was the only key to that dead bolt.

"Bye, Mommie. Bye, Daddy!" Kimmy called.

"All right, kiddo," I said, turning to her. "You heard Mom. Time for bed." She hesitated. "Go on now, I'll get your pineapple juice for you." At nine years of age my sister was a pineapple-juice-at-bedtime addict. I watched her gulp down her "fix," then tucked her in.

I settled under the covers of my bed and picked up Volume A of the encyclopedia I had been reading; I could see Kim asleep across the suite.

"Come, Houdi!" The little white poodle jumped up and curled into a knot at my feet.

The hours went by quickly. Then, footsteps. Mother's sharp high heels followed by Papa's heavy tread thudded down the six stairs that divided the living room from the bedrooms. Houdi sprang up and began growling softly. The high heels stopped at my mother's room. The door was yanked open, then slammed shut. Then my father's footsteps stopped at his room; that door was also jerked open then slammed. Kimmy sat up, startled, and rubbed her eyes. "Oh," she murmured, "Mommy and Daddy are home," and fell back to sleep.

"That's odd," I thought. "I didn't hear the gate open. Oh, shut up, Houdi!" The little dog was still growling on the bed. Outside I could hear Hungry frantically howling and barking. "Cows must be on the street again," I thought as I got out of bed and went into the hall. I opened the door to father's room to say goodnight.

"Dad?" I called, "Daddy?" He wasn't there. "Probably out in the garden," I reasoned. I knocked at my mother's room. No answer. It was empty. There was no way she could have gone past me.

"Something's not right," I said softly, suddenly frightened. I hurried back to my room and picked up the gun.

"Come, Houdi!" The little dog jumped off the bed and followed me to the door. He stopped at the threshold and, snarling viciously, backed away, refusing to go further. Kim whimpered softly in her sleep and tossed restlessly under the covers.

I stepped into the hall and walked up the stairs, the gun heavy in my hand. I reached the top and stopped. I felt a dead, clammy chill as if I had stepped suddenly into a giant ice box filled with dead fish. The presence of something evil permeated the air and I began to shiver. *The front door was standing wide open.*

"Mom? Daddy?" Silence but for the continuous howling of the dog outside. I walked hesitantly across the room and shut the door. Soft, low laughter began to echo in my head, a kind of laughter I had never heard before and which filled me with terror. Slowly, deliberately, I moved into a corner chair and pointed my gun towards the door. I looked down at my watch: 11:20 p.m.

Thirty-five minutes later a car turned into our driveway. I heard the sound of the heavy metal gate being pushed open then pulled shut as the engine was shut off inside the carport. I sat in my chair and waited, gun pointed at the door.

"Hungry, will you cut out that racket!" Papa shouted. "There's not a cow in sight, you stupid dog." I could hear him fumbling through his keys.

I ran to the door and flung it open, the gun still in my hand. "What the...!" he exclaimed surprised, and then, "Was someone trying to get in? Are you all right?"

My heart was still pounding in my throat, but my

words were slow and deliberate as I told him what had happened.

"Someone must have broken in and been frightened away," he said when I finished.

"But Daddy, Kim and I both heard your footsteps and the doors slam!" I protested, "and I heard someone laughing at me!"

"You've really let your imagination run away with you tonight," he answered gruffly. "Just put it out of your mind now and go to bed." He relocked the door and went downstairs.

Papa was a New Yorker, and despite having produced the first Inner Sanctum mysteries on radio he was still pragmatic when confronted with something of this nature in his own home.

"Mama, I didn't make it up. Something else has moved in. Can't you feel it?" I looked up at her anxiously.

Mama said nothing, but hugged me close for a long while.

❀

The being who moved into our home that night was not a pleasant one. He seemed to take a grim delight in frightening me. One night, several days after his arrival, I awoke suddenly from a deep sleep. A voice was groaning softly as though in pain. My eyes shot open. There, at the end of my bed, suspended in mid-air, floated a grotesque head, severed, oozing blood and gore at the neck. The thick black hair and heavy beard were matted with blood and the mouth hung limp and open letting the groans escape it. I lay still, paralyzed with fear, my eyes fixed on the apparition. Then the groans changed to a soft, deep laugh that slowly faded with the head.

On other nights I would walk into my room and see

a severed arm, dark and hairy, lying on my pillow. After a few seconds it would fade away, while the same slow laughter surrounded me.

Over the years several maids quit and many refused to spend the night in our house, saying that "something gave fright" in it. Yet it apparently never manifested itself to Mom and Dad.

There are other memories of those years—happier memories of trips to the local pyramids to collect arrowheads and rocks, of hugging soft kittens and romping through lush green gardens with assorted dogs as we "helped Mama" tend to her hibiscus bushes. There were days spent in the sunshine by the pool with Daddy and lively games of checkers in which he sometimes let me beat him. And I will never forget the sound of Mama's faint Georgia accent, barely perceptible as she read from *Charlotte's Webb* or *Stuart Little*, but which burst forth in all its unintelligible glory when confronted with the Southern-fried tales of Uncle Remus. To her great disappointment, she never got past the first few pages with us, and I was a sophomore in college before I finally figured out what a "Bre'r Rabbit" was.

I also remember ballet classes, enchanting but for a broken leg acquired at the age of seven while practicing fire-bird leaps in the garden after rehearsal one evening, and the memory of a flubbed recital which is best left unrecounted.

But mostly I remember the nuns.

The then austerely garbed sisters of the Sacred Heart of Mary arrived in Cuernavaca in time for me to be enrolled in the third grade. The nuns were formidable in their habits and seemed to move about the antique panelled halls and marble columns of the school in an aura of untouchable dignity and holiness, an illusion further enforced by mandatory curtsies to be rendered at every encounter.

Underneath the blanket of that impression lived warm, caring women who, for the most part, did their best to prepare us for the world in general and college in particular, in light of which I will forever bitterly resent having been forced to graduate the year before Sister Sarah taught her World Literature class.

4
Turning Point

Bishop Pike and his family spent a month in Cuernavaca in 1963, the summer I was fourteen.

The Senior Warden of our church to whom the privilege of hosting the Bishop would normally have fallen was ill, so the task fell on Daddy, the Junior Warden of St. Michaels.

The two families seemed to take an immediate liking to one another and spent a good deal of time together during that month. I remember lively evenings in our home during which the Bishop discussed the subject matter of some complex book he was writing while Father offered highly creative, if not altogether appropriate suggestions for titles.

The Bishop brought three of his children with him. Connie, a year or so older that I, was attractive, slender and very popular with the American boys who had come home from school for the summer. The Bishop's two sons fell into the typical "preacher's kids" category. Chris was thirteen and didn't seem to like me in particular. He once took my finger and twisted it until I cried. The more disturbing of the two, however, was Jim. At seventeen he had a dark, brooding air, which could erupt easily into violence when he had been drinking. It was hard for me to understand what seemed to be such overt rebellion and dramatic public outbursts. I was frightened of him, yet felt a strange affinity for him. I sensed in him the same unanswered cry for help I carried within myself. I thought of him frequently during the next few years.

In February of 1966 young Jim was dead. He shot himself while on drugs in a New York hotel. His death and the widely publicized display of psychic phenomena which followed proved to be a turning point in my life. My heart leaped when I heard that the Bishop was attending seances in order to contact his dead son. I wasn't the only one experiencing bizarre phenomena! Perhaps in the Bishop's search I would find the key that would help me understand and deal with the beings who surrounded me.

I now eagerly read any book or article I could find on the occult. Strange dreams of myself in different forms and different places came to me as I slept and I would hear a voice within my mind tell me these were memories of different incarnations.

My thoughts were filled with death and the peace it could bring. There were times I felt imprisoned by my body almost as though I had been dropped into it by mistake, and I yearned to be free of it, although I never would have dared to take my own life. The deeper I studied, the more aware I became of the spirits' almost tangible companionship; not all seemed to be evil. I saw dark figures by my bed, heard their soft voices calling to me, telling me what people were thinking, thoughts which often betrayed what their mouths were saying.

The resulting distrust and dislike I felt for most people gradually deepened into solid contempt. Yet my feelings were generally masked in such outward composure and serenity that an old Spanish priest once called me a "mystic." There was only one person I trusted—a wonderful little Mexican nun named Mother Bernardo. She reached out to me as one might to a frightened kitten. Her concern and companionship made the black depression of my last two years of high school almost bearable.

During this time school had become little more than a necessary evil. I plodded through my classes, having basically lost interest in anything that was taught. I performed because it was expected.

Then one day during my senior year in high school, the subject of witchcraft was brought up in class. Was it real? Most of the girls expressed skepticism. "Mere superstition," one girl commented. "Totally stupid," said another.

"How can you be sure?" I finally queried, frustrated by what I viewed as shallow ignorance. "There is another dimension surrounding us—closer to us than we think—filled with beings of a different kind. Is it so improbable that there are those who see them and have, perhaps, learned the secret of harnessing these forces? Perhaps even some of us here are learning to do that," I added softly. There was an uncomfortable pause before the nun in charge of the class cleared her throat and dismissed us for our break.

"Wait, Johanna!" Terry*, who had left the class moments after I had, was calling to me down the hall. "I need to ask you—These powers you were talking about—Can they get something back for me? Do they really work?"

"What do you mean, Terry?" I asked.

"Well, I know you'll think this is silly," she laughed nervously. "My boyfriend and I broke up last week. Can you help me get him back?"

It so happened that just the day before I had read of a young English girl—a witch, who had been faced with the same problem. She performed a strange ritual alone, deep in the forest, using two clay dolls she made, a magic circle, a short wooden stake and a fresh, raw sheep's heart. Mysterious incantations completed the ritual. Her boyfriend, for better or worse, was back within the week. Frankly, it seemed a bit extreme to me; witchcraft was something I had always been afraid of because of what to me were its obvious satanic overtones. I read about it as I came across material on the subject, but I never explored it in depth. Besides, a lot of the ritual struck me as being somewhat ridiculous and overstated. But if Terry needed a ritual and was desperate enough to think a boyfriend worth the effort, then why should I stand in her way. I described the ritual in great detail, smiling to myself as she gasped at the mention of the sheep's heart, but she said she would do it.

That weekend I received a call from Terry. All was ready. Just one small problem, though—this business about the sheep's heart. Was that really necessary? It was...Oh...Well then, could I help her locate one.

"Certainly not. You must find it yourself. That's part of the ritual," I told her, admitting inwardly that the sheep's heart was every bit as repulsive to me as it was to her. I was amazed that she was actually planning to go through with the whole ordeal.

Terry tried for days to coax me into helping her. What had initially amused me was now beginning to irritate me. Finally one morning I turned to her, interrupting another of her pleas for help, and said, "Terry, you've been bothering me with this long enough. You would do better to leave me alone and to watch out for your hands!"

"What do you mean?" she gasped as she stepped back.

"Nothing," I said crossly, wondering why I had said

anything in the first place. "Just leave me alone."

The next day Terry arrived at school late; her hands were stained a deep purple-black. The skin up to the forearms had been scrubbed and scoured until it was raw and angry looking. The explanation was simple enough: She had been dying a friend's hair the night before and the gloves had leaked. But the look on her face plainly said she felt I had hexed her and was to blame. In any case, it was the last I heard of the sheep's heart.

Later, however, several of her friends approached me in the hall. One of them suddenly held up a cross to my face with all the earnestness of Doctor Von Helsing before the countenance of Dracula, just to see if I, perhaps, was a true witch after all and would fall writhing to the floor at the sight.

Ironically, it was the cross I clung to in the midst of the agonizing loneliness and despair I felt closing in on me from every side.

As for Terry, she dropped the subject altogether, but when I contracted infectious hepatitis in an epidemic at the school a month later, she sent a note on a card joking (somewhat nervously) about the hex she had placed on me in revenge.

5
Wesleyan

"You fool!" I muttered angrily to myself, "When will you ever learn to keep your mouth shut!" I was standing on the far shore of the little lake which lay at the foot of the campus. The woods stood thick and dark behind me as the sun dropped slowly out of sight, the cue for countless frogs and crickets to begin their nightly recital. I had not been at Wesleyan College in Macon, Georgia three weeks before I again succeeded in having myself labeled the one thing I knew I was not—a witch.

On that first day of class, Dr. Bryce* paced up and down the room critically eyeing the freshman troop of would-be actresses and directors who sat before her.

"Girls, be assured of one thing: You will work hard in this class—very hard indeed or heads will *roll.*" The look in her eyes as her faint Dutch accent drew out the "r" in "roll" left no doubt in anyone's mind that she was quite capable of literally carrying out her threat. "Now," she continued, "if you're determined to be in theater despite that fact, you must learn to develop your bodies and minds, such as they are," she added wryly. "But most of all, you must expand the one thing without which not one of you belongs in the theater:

Imagination! You must become interested in all that which stimulates your imagination, in that which is different...even mysterious..."

"Like the occult, Dr. Bryce?" The words were out of my mouth before I could stop them.

Dr. Bryce stopped, then turned and stared at me for a moment, as did the rest of the class. "Perhaps," she said slowly, raising a quizzical eyebrow at me. "Perhaps."

Several days later I was sitting in the theater waiting for the compulsory weekly chapel service to begin. Some girls from my acting class sat next to me and began speaking about Dr. Bryce—what a fascinating person she was, what a fabulous sense of humor she had, how exciting her class was proving to be.

"By the way," one of the girls said, "just what did you mean when you mentioned the occult in class the other day? Do you know much about it?"

"Oh, a little," I answered, pleased by the sudden attention and respect I saw on their faces. "Perhaps these girls will understand," I thought naively, "not like the others in Mexico."

"Please, tell us. We really want to know!"

So I shared a bit about the being I had seen and joked, unfairly, about poor Terry and her credulity. My audience was with me all the way. Then one girl asked if I could cure warts. There was an enormous one on the finger she held in front of me.

"Surely she's not serious," I thought. "Well," I answered with a laugh, "it's not my specialty, but I'll see what I can do. Just give it a couple of weeks." Our conversation ended as the lights in the auditorium dimmed and the chapel service began.

I forgot the whole thing until one afternoon two weeks later when I was accosted by a girl with a strange expression on her face. She looked vaguely familiar but I couldn't remember who she was—"Thanks, Johanna, thanks very much."

"You're entirely welcome. For what?"

"My wart—the one you said you'd work on, it's *gone!* It fell off last night, and within the two weeks. Thanks a lot!"

The awe in her voice was unmistakable. I looked down at her extended finger. Sure enough. The silly thing, which I now remembered vividly, was indeed gone. I knew I had nothing to do with it, but if she wanted to think I had, that was fine with me. "Well, how nice for you," I said, smiling cryptically.

Word of my power over protruberant viral appendages (that's "warts" to you) spread quickly through the campus, and "witchcraft" came to be the most likely explanation for what had occurred. After all, I did dress mostly in black and spent long hours walking alone in the woods collecting mysterious herbs and leaves (used as decorations on my desk), and I *did* have a statue of Mephistopheles on my dresser, (a gift from my parents' shop and a takeoff on my mother's graduate school motto: "He must needs go whom the devil driveth") and I did speak of the occult to Dr. Bryce on the first day of class. Besides, it was obvious she liked me (that alone might have sufficed to build their case against me). Then, of course, there was the matter of the subject of my freshman term paper. I had elected to write on voodooism in Haiti—an unfortunate choice, I will admit, but then it was the only interesting subject I could think of at the time. Worst of all, I was in theater and loved cats. What more proof could anyone ask for? Witchcraft was the only possible answer. (By now I had collected a small group of partisans who reported these conversations to me.)

My initial reaction of frustration to all this began to give way to amusement. "Let the fools think what they like," I thought. "God knows I'm not a witch. I know I'm psychic; I know I can develop strange powers if I put my mind to it, but I'm not a witch. It is rather fun to watch them squirm, though."

In any case, at least the being who had made my life a constant misery in Mexico seemed to have been left behind. It had been over a month since I had been aware of its presence. Perhaps I would never see it again. The prospect of that made me breathe a little easier.

Then it happened.

❋

It was cold and silent in the theater that October evening. Everyone on campus had gone to dinner. I had been working for over five hours straight and was tired, but decided to work overtime in order to complete some props needed for rehearsal that night. Dr. Bryce had appointed me properties mistress for the first show of the year, an original musical. I did not wish to incur her inimitable "heads will roll" invective which I knew, however much she might like me, would be forthcoming if the "realistic" gray fish needed for the monger's stall were not ready. The forfeit of hot dinner seemed a small price to pay for the keeping of my head.

The tiny workshop behind the enormous stage was filled with the stench of stock paint simmering on the burner. I switched it off and gave a final stir to the bubbling grey brew. There. Just a few more touches and those mackerel would fool anyone at thirty paces. I turned to reach for my brush and stopped. The temperature in the room suddenly dropped. I shivered. I glanced around the room to see if perhaps I had left a window open. They were all shut. Then I heard a voice—soft and menacing, hissing in my ear. "What are you doing here—this is *my* time. What are you doing here—Get out!" I whirled around. There was no one there. Then the voice seemed to be coming from the stage: *"Get out—this is my time."*

I stepped out onto the dark stage: "Who's there?" I called, still shivering.

Then I saw a large glowing ball of light pulsating slowly in the darkness at center stage. The woman's voice came again, screaming hysterically now. "What are you doing here—This is *my* time—GET OUT!"

"I'm sorry, I'm sorry. I didn't know this was your time. I'm leaving." My voice was soothing and conciliatory, for I instinctively sensed I would be in great danger if I showed the panic I felt. I turned and walked slowly down the steps that led from the stage into the auditorium. As I reached the back of the auditorium, the voice from the pulsing light screamed again. "GET OUT!"

I turned and ran into the hall and pushed my way through the heavy doors that led to the courtyard outside. I was halfway across the courtyard when I felt an icy stare cut through my back. I glanced over my shoulder and whirled around. There, in the doorway through which I had just come, stood a woman in a long white dress. She stared at me for a moment and then threw her head back and laughed. I turned and ran.

There was scarcely a time when I was in that theater alone (a situation I now avoided as much as possible) that I didn't hear the same shrill laughter, usually accompanied by loud footsteps or the sound of rustling skirts. There were times when others with me sensed that same presence. Donna, a fellow acting student, was one of those.

We had both been cast in Enid Bagnold's *The Chalk*

Garden. One evening a few days before tryouts I felt a sudden compulsion to draw vine leaves. When I read the play and saw that Madrigal, the protagonist, spent many hours drawing vine leaves on altar candles, I knew the part would be mine even though I wasn't much of an actress. I spent so many years feeling I was not part of my body and wanting to disassociate myself from it, that now when I needed to convey to an audience the inner being and soul of the character I was portraying, it refused to respond with ease to my command. I was having an especially difficult time making myself heard in the back rows, so this night Donna offered to stay after rehearsal and help me work on my projection.

The curtains on stage had been drawn shut. I stood on the wide apron, center stage, while Donna settled into a seat in the back of the theater. We had been working on a scene for several minutes when I heard a sound like a sigh and soft footsteps directly behind me on the other side of the curtain. The feeling someone was about to reach out through the part in the curtains and place a hand on my shoulder was overwhelming. Abruptly I spun around and flung aside the folds. "Who's there?" I called. As the curtains parted, Donna and I saw a filmy white figure retreat into the darkness. Then soft footsteps and a softer high pitched laugh like the one I had heard before echoed as it withdrew. That was the last time Donna offered to work late with me in the theater.

I tried to appease the hatred of this phantom woman with offerings. Several times I gathered small bouquets of colorful leaves and wild flowers which I left on stage for her. "Here...I've brought you these. Please, can't we be friends...?" My gifts were greeted with icy silence. Then fear and anger would swirl around me in almost tangible waves and I knew my gift had been rejected.

❀

Thanksgiving came quickly that first year at Wesleyan. I spent it with my mother's sister, Dorothea, and her family. Aunt Dot in her warm, gentle manner immediately made me feel at home. To ease the trauma of my first holiday spent away from my parents, she gave me a gift, a Ouija board. "After all," she joked in her gentle Georgia accent, "everyone who does a term paper on voodooism should have one!"

I was delighted with the board. I heard of it through my studies but still had not realized how easily they were obtained in the States. As soon as I returned to Wesleyan I showed the board to Katy* and Jill*, who roomed together down the hall. They were as eager as I to try it, as was my roommate, Ruth*. We spent many hours working the board in a dimly lit room. The sense of a presence would surround us—then the marker would begin spelling out messages. It was all amusing and seemed quite innocent until one evening the presence that arrived was overwhelming in its feeling of evil. The water pipes in the room began to bang loudly and bright lights seemed to flash at the doorway. I looked up and saw the same misty white-garbed woman I had seen at the theater.

That experience, plus the fact that some ugly predictions which the board had made about one of the girls present had very nearly come true, frightened me so badly that I vowed never to use the board again. There was something dangerous and sinister about it. It was no innocent toy.

I had sworn all the participants in the board experiments to silence, but, not surprisingly, word of the strange occurrences spread through the campus. My reputation was rapidly moving from "questionable" to "positively dreadful." A girl had run screaming hysterically from her room one night when her roommate pinned a black "J" (ostensibly for "Johanna") on her pillow as a joke. She was certain I had hexed her and she would die. Girls would spot me coming down the hall of certain dorms, and doors would slam on either side.

Early one morning a friend awoke to see me standing outside her window. She was about to ask me in, when she suddenly realized her window was on the second floor. I was in my room at the time, asleep. In my dream I could see her lying in bed, awakening with a start as she looked out her window.

Unfortunately, the president of the college heard of the commotion, of which I seemed to be the source. One morning I passed him in the cafeteria. "Ah . . . good morning, Johanna."

"Good morning, Sir," I answered politely.

"Ah . . . I hear you're indulging in the powers of the occult, my deah" he drawled. "Are you sure that's wise?" His question hit me like a bucket of ice water.

"Why, I'm really not doing anything of the kind," I protested, smiling as innocently as I could manage.

"Well, that's not what I hear. You be careful now. Good day," he said as he backed out the door.

I heard later from an upperclassman that several girls had been expelled for attending witches' sabbaths down by the lake several years before I arrived. They claimed responsibility for an unusually severe hailstorm which pummeled the campus shortly after their dismissal, so it was understandable if the president was somewhat fidgety about the subject.

❋

After two years at Wesleyan I was ready, or so I imagined, for a change. I was tired of leading men, recruited from the art department or the Air Force base, who gulped tranquilizers on opening night and then proceeded to ad lib the entire script. I also wanted additional courses in directing and makeup. Most of all I wanted a sense of freedom. Life for me at Wesleyan had become as stifling as that in Mexico, where every move was watched and accounted for lest my reputation be permanently maimed. So I applied for a transfer to the University of North Carolina at Chapel Hill, and was accepted.

I knew I would miss Dr. Bryce and the evenings spent discussing theater, listening to Rachmaninoff, Von Williams, and Tchaikovsky, but I had to move.

I certainly was to find the "freedom" I wanted, but as far as any further progress in theater it was the worst move I could have made.

6
Chapel Hill

I stepped inside the quaint, peaceful theater and looked down at the stage. How different this theater and the whole campus were from what I had left behind at Wesleyan. I walked down to the stage, placed my hands on the ledge and looked across to the wood floorboard. "This is the place I will haunt when I die," I said to myself softly. No melodrama—just a statement of fact. "You won't mind will you?" As I spoke, I became aware of another presence in the theater, as though my words startled someone out of a deep sleep. Yet the feeling, unexpectedly, was warm and embracing—so unlike the cold hatred of the being at Wesleyan. Tears ran down my face. I had finally come home.

Nevertheless, the transition to Chapel Hill was not an easy one. Coed classes were strange to me. In acting class especially, I blossomed into a prime example of how a suddenly uncovered gamut of inhibitions can stifle a performance. My acting coach seemed to think playing the part of a nymphomaniac, and hurtling defiant and obscene raspberries at the class, would somehow break the barrier of my "hangups." He was wrong. It was obvious to me Professor Benecroft* felt my presence in acting class was a pitiful mistake. All the confidence I had sensed from Dr. Bryce in my growing ability vanished. What talent I had was not enough to overcome a growing sense of defeat.

Well, what did it matter? I had known for several months that I would probably never go into acting as a career. I wanted to change to a directing major but was unable to do so because of the way the program was set up at the time. All the courses I had hoped to take when I made my decision to leave Wesleyan were now unavailable to me. So acting became a cover, an excuse. I could give full reign to my eccentricities (I had come to accept them as such) and knew few people would question them. After all, I was "in the theater." Who knows what strange role I might be rehearsing!

"In a world of water who can tell when goldfish weep."

Nevertheless, I found a small group of people whose company I enjoyed. The theater brought a number of us into a special bond—a kind of secret brotherhood.

After rehearsals we would sometimes gather in Jack* and Adam's* room on the top floor of Graham Memorial, our theater building, to smoke pot or hash and talk. I didn't even know what pot was until now, but in my new surroundings it seemed innocent enough.

It was an interesting group. Jack was an acting major. Despite his determination to play Richard III he was kind and gentle. He had a good singing voice and I enjoyed watching his craggy, serious face as he bent over his guitar.

Adam, his roommate, was in tech and had the most marvelous auburn hair I had ever seen.

And there was Kevan*—tall, blue-eyed with a wry half-smile I found very appealing. One morning not long after I arrived at Chapel Hill, Kevan informed me that some of the guys had consulted the Ouija board about me. "Well," he said, smiling sheepishly, ". . . you've shared so little about yourself and have such a mysterious air about you, they got curious." I had learned to keep my mouth shut since Wesleyan.

"And what did it tell them?" I asked, surprised. It never occurred to me they would even know what a Ouija board was.

Kevan blushed a bit and stammered, "Well, it, it said you are the incarnation of a priestess from another planet . . . and, um . . . that you have strange powers which you're just beginning to discover, that you know a strange written language, and that you can see auras and astral project. Actually, everyone is just a little afraid of you."

I said nothing. It sounded ridiculous when he said it, but what the board had told them was astonishingly close to what I had felt about myself for many years.

"Well," he insisted half laughing, "Is it true?"

"If that's what people want to think, there's nothing I can say," I replied. "But if I were you, I'd keep away from Ouija boards. They can be dangerous." I thought back on my own board, hidden away in the bottom of my trunk. I gave Kevan a side-long glance as we continued walking, evaluating him in a new light. It was obvious his knowledge of metaphysics was limited, but at least he had the nerve to come directly to me with his questions. Perhaps I had found a friend who would understand.

Beck* was part of the group also. He reminded me of a portrait I had once seen of Shakespeare, with his large brown eyes, long hair, and high forehead. Beck liked me, but I kept him at arm's length for well over a year. "Someday you'll find you need me," he said. "I can wait."

And there was Damon*, perhaps the most talented

actor to go through Playmakers in a long time. Damon—dark, brooding, intense—reminded me of myself. "If I were a man, I'd probably be like Damon," I thought when I first saw him. He had a girlfriend, a lovely dark-haired girl, and that disappointed me. I knew I would probably never get a chance to know him.

As much as I liked our group I never felt really comfortable with them, and I turned to the being in the theater for true companionship. I could sense his presence even though there had not yet been any physical manifestation. I called him "Professor Koch" after the founder of Playmakers.

Then, late one night, the summons came. I was awakened by dark figures standing by my bed, whispering, murmuring, beckoning me to the theater. I rose, dressed quietly so as not to awaken Paula*, my roommate, and ran through the arboretum and across the silent campus to the theater. I had managed to obtain my own key to Playmakers within weeks of arriving at Chapel Hill. I slipped into the dark hall, pulled the doors shut behind me, then ran up the few steps to the light switch. Soft lights filled the theater. I sat on the steps by the stage and waited, knowing I had been summoned, but still not certain why. Minutes passed, then I heard the inner swinging panels at the front entrance begin hitting against the locked doors. The sound stopped as abruptly as it had begun. Silence.

Then a two-dimensional, hazy figure of a man with thick grey hair and dressed in dark striped pants and a white shirt with an odd little tie appeared at the door. He paused and looked at me for a moment—then drifted towards me. He stopped halfway down the aisle, sat in a seat, and looked at me again. I said nothing. There was no need. I sensed he knew all I was thinking, all the expectation tinged with fear I was experiencing. A melody filled the theater—urgent, beautiful, a song of unrestrained longing and loneliness. The melody, in minor key like an old Hebrew desert song, rose and fell and spoke to me of the serenity of death. Then I realized my voice had become the instrument for that melody, that it was coming through my mouth, that it had become my own. When the song had run its course I stood, opened my eyes and looked again at Professor Koch. He smiled at me, then faded quietly from my sight. The gift of the song had been given. It was time to leave.

❊

Several days later, the Little People made their appearance. They stood 1½-2 feet high, transparent as Professor Koch, dressed in green and brown. Their small ugly faces were plump, ruddy and their eyes twinkled as they peeked out at me from behind a wood pile at the theater workshop. Frequently four or five of them accompanied me on the walks I took through the mossy graveyard planted just behind my dormitory. They never spoke—just played and romped and made me smile. Yet sometimes, unlike the certainty of what I saw in the theater, I wondered if I really saw them—if they were really there.

7
Damon

The harsh ring of the phone startled me, and my head turned sharply towards the sound. Several candles stood lit about the room casting strange, undulating shadows on the walls. The sweet aroma of myrrh and frankincense burning on a small coal filled my head. The ring came a second time. I turned from the dresser where I had been standing, and lifted the receiver off its hook.

"Johanna, is that you?"

"Yes."

"This is Damon. I need to talk to you. May I come over now?"

"Of course." My tone did not convey the surprise I felt.

"I'll be there in ten minutes."

I hung up and went back to the ancient clay figure standing on my dresser.

"Tiresias, did you hear, Damon is coming. What does he want, I wonder. He has spoken to me only a few times, but I've felt him watch me with those dark eyes of his. How strange that he should call."

I stared into the blind slits of the small pre-Columbian fire-god's eyes. His deformed, bald head tilted forward as he sat cross-legged, his chin resting on his hands. His mouth curved upward in a mirthful knowing smirk. He looked wise and ancient, this "old man with wrinkled dugs...who sat by Thebes below the wall and walked among the lowest of the dead."[1]

Tiresias, the ancient prophet, was purchased from an old medicine man in Cuernavaca when I was fifteen. Tiresias gave me my "language" one night while still at Wesleyan as I sat staring at him in the flickering candlelight—an unspoken language half Chinese, half Arabic in appearance, which, when written, could express every emotion, every raging passion of a soul, which was unable or, perhaps, just too afraid to translate its surging life into the spoken word. And the longing and hope and love that I wrote I surrounded with the vines I first drew for Madrigal—thick, full vines from which these fragile feelings could draw their strength so that they would not die before they were fulfilled.

There was a soft knock on the door before it swung open. A tall, thin figure with piercing, strangely slanted eyes stood in the hallway. A faint half-smile played about the corners of his lips. He carried a long black cape which he was using for his performance as Count Dracula, the current Playmakers' production.

"Damon—come in."

He paused for a moment, then stepped into the dimly lit room, filling it with a dark mysterious presence.

"Come, there's someone you should meet." I took him to the dresser. "Tiresias, this is Damon." I lifted Tiresias to greet him face to face. "And *he*," I pointed to the grinning carved-wood devil by the candles, "is Mephistopheles." Then with a low laugh, I added, "He must needs go whom the devil driveth."

"Do devils drive you, Johanna?"

I met his gaze and said nothing.

---

[1] T.S. Eliot—*The Wasteland*, p. 36, Faber and Faber, LTD. MCMXL.

He stared intently at me for several seconds, then drew something out of his pocket—two small lumps of tin foil—and placed them on the dresser in front of Tiresias.

"I've brought this for you." I looked up at him.

"It's mescaline," he said in answer to my silent question. "Will you take it with me?" The slant of his eyes in the candlelight gave his face a strange, foreign look.

"Please," he said softly, "it's important." I picked up a cup, filled it with water at the sink in the corner of the room, and placed it by the two small lumps on the dresser.

He carefully unwrapped the tablets and handed me one. A faint bitter taste hit the back of my throat as I swallowed it. I passed the cup to Damon and watched as he placed the second white tablet in his mouth and swallowed.

"Put your cape on. It's cold outside and we'll be walking." I reached for my long black cape and pulled it on over my head as Damon hung his massive cape around his shoulders.

We stepped outside into the crisp clear Carolina night and made our way across campus. Within minutes the entire world seemed transported to a fairy land where tiny diamonds flashed and sparkled and burst into multi-colored flames everywhere I looked. What awesome beauty was around me. I felt as though at any second my spirit would be lifted from my body and flung open-armed into the sparkling universe around me, never to return. We made our way to Graham Memorial. Jack and Adam weren't home.

We stepped back out into the glossy darkness. And I was flying, set free at last from this body which had shackled me to earth. I looked down at myself walking beside Damon and wondered what it was that kept my body gliding there beside him.

We floated through the night for hours—or

minutes—I'm not sure, but suddenly I opened my eyes and we were in the graveyard. Damon moved ahead of me. He no longer was a talented actor rehearsing the role of Count Dracula in his long black cape. He *was* Dracula. I looked about me as I walked and the rocks became faces with flesh that shriveled and fell away leaving only skulls with gaping eyes and screaming mouths. I forced my mind to see the rocks I knew were there. Damon stopped beside a crumbling gravestone. He turned and looked at me, his eyes hard and cold, the half-smile on his white face ghastly. Then he slowly bent to the ground and stretched himself out along the grave and folded his arms upon his chest. I stood by the grave next to him and then lay down beside him, also like one dead.

I could hear voices all around me, voices that I had heard at other times while in the graveyard. Only now, somehow, they were clearer, less distant, and they were sobbing, mourning the death of a beloved. Their voices seemed to mingle oddly with the cries of those long caught within their graves, lamenting their imprisonment. The voice beneath my body groaned and whimpered and pressed within the confines of its coffin. Could it be that even in death there was no peace? I thought there would be peace.

"Oh, God, God—help me. I'm alone, and so afraid." The voices seemed to hush around me and once again grew far away and distant, as though the final tired winds of some spent hurricane had carried them out to sea.

I opened my eyes and turned my head. Damon was still lying on his grave. Then his eyes flew open and he sat up, slowly, stood and without a word turned to leave the place of death.

We found our way back to Graham Hall. It was an hour before dawn and we were both coming down from the drug. "Let's sit here for a while." Damon sank down on the stairs which lead to the second floor of the building. The heavy cape slid off his shoulders. Exhausted, drained of energy and emotion, I sat on the stairs beside him.

Then, after a pause, "Why, Damon, why all of this?"

"It's simple, really," he answered. "I want to get to know you and a trip like this is one the fastest ways I know to cut through all the crap."

"What do you mean?" I asked.

"I'm talking about you, Johanna. You've built a fortress around yourself. In the four months you've been here no one seems to have really gotten to know you."

"I know. That's the way I've wanted it."

"Why, in God's name? All kinds of strange stories are going around about you, do you know that? People think you're out of your mind. You've even got some of the guys in tech believing you're a priestess from another planet and have strange powers."

I smiled. "Yes. So Kevan told me."

"And this thing about Tiresias giving you a language and your Little People—just what kind of a game are you playing, Johanna?"

"Game?" I asked softly, surprised by the word. "Is it a game? I don't know sometimes, Damon. I know some think I'm insane—or on the very edge at least, I've seen it in their faces when they look at me. You know, sometimes I find myself smiling at their blindness, their gullibility, cunning and plotting how I can best make use of that belief. And suddenly I stop, frightened by my own deviousness."

My voice was tired, far away. "Maybe they're right; maybe I am insane. I really feel as though I don't belong in this world, as though I had been created for another dimension, a sparkling, radiant world where I could fly and soar into the air with my people and serve upon the altar of my God. Do you ever have the feeling you're not really part of your body, that you were dropped into it by mistake?" Damon was looking intently at me but said nothing. "I do," I continued. "I feel trapped in this body. There is more beyond this life, Damon. There are spirit beings all around us. I can see them, hear them. I feel when they are near calling to me—but sometimes I'm so afraid of them. There is an awful evil which comes among them sometimes. They've come to me ever since I was little. They *are* there, Damon, others have seen them with me, heard them. But Tiresias and my Little People...I don't know. Perhaps I've been so lonely my own mind has created them. I'm so frightened sometimes, Damon. Oh, God, if I could only find peace within myself."

Damon said nothing for many minutes. His face was composed, but his eyes reflected a soul—trapped and screaming—searching frantically for the soothing, healing waters of peace—searching with no real hope of ever finding what couldn't long be lived without. I recognized the look.

It was my own.

8
Angry Shadows

In April I decided to adopt a snake. I made this momentous decision while I was still nursing several badly bruised ribs acquired by falling off the stage at Ford's Theater in Washington D.C. on the 27th of March, 1971.

We had entered the American College Theater Festival months before with an unusual production of an old German play called *Woyzeck*. Our show was selected one of the ten best out of 240 colleges all over the country, a fact which gave us the honor of performing at Ford's Theater.

Opening night the lights dimmed on cue at the end of the fourth scene and then unexpectedly blacked out. I got turned around in the darkness and walked straight off the end of the stage. Somehow I landed on the only flat unit in the orchestra pit. If I had gone several inches in either direction I would have tripped over a footlight and landed on the edge of some open unit which quite possibly would have killed me. As it was, the fall knocked my breath out. The pain on my right side was paralyzing, so I simply lay there for about fifteen minutes wondering if I could be seen from the front rows. I hoped not. All the critics were in the front rows.

When I had caught my breath, I pulled myself back on stage during another scene change and finished the show.

Several years later I saw a newspaper article which mentioned that many performers had suffered strange accidents on that stage, especially in the path Booth had followed in his attempted escape after Lincoln's assassination. Where I had fallen was directly in the path shown on their diagram.

Mama flew in from Mexico to take care of me. I don't know how I would have made it through that time without her. There was no more comforting hand in the world to me than my mother's.

After several weeks I was able to fend for myself again and she returned to Mexico. That was when I decided to adopt a snake (not as a replacement for my mother, I hasten to add). Besides, rehearsing Cleopatra's death scene for acting class without the benefit of an asp seemed futile. And Professor Benecroft said live props were always helpful. Oddly enough, Barney's Animal Kingdom pet store was fresh out of asps. They did, however, have a beguiling South American baby boa. He was only 19 inches long and had the loveliest pattern on his back, so I named him Quetzalcoatl and took him home around my neck.

On the way to my dorm I ran into Adam. He was enthralled with my new pet and immediately proceeded to the workshop. After almost two hours of sawing and hammering, he presented the creature with a wooden cage. It had a leather shoulder strap so I could carry him with me, and a screen on one side so he could look out. It was fully equipped with a little tub of water and tree branch.

Reactions to my pet were varied. He was either immediately accepted and cuddled or, more frequently, greeted with short shrieks of ghastly recognition—as, for example, in the case of one teacher with whom I stopped to talk one afternoon. The days were still cold so, as usual, I let the thing wrap himself around my neck to keep warm.

In the middle of the conversation she stopped to admire my necklace. "My, isn't that an unusual piece of jewelry you're wearing." Her fingers reached out to sample the unfamiliar texture. Quetzalcoatl lifted his head and flicked his little tongue at her. The ensuing scream turned heads halfway across campus.

My rendition of Cleopatra improved not at all with the acquisition of the baby boa, but it did start a fad on campus that lasted several months. More important to me, however, Quetzalcoatl was something alive to care for and love.

Many, I know, will refuse to believe this, but boas have lovely personalities—well, South American boas anyway. Central American boas have ticks and bite. Over a period of weeks he learned to recognize my scent with his flicking tongue and would make his way across my desk to wrap himself around my arm—something he did for no one else. (Of course there may have been no one else he wanted to throttle, either.)

Granted, a snake was a far cry from my first choice for a pet. I would infinitely have preferred a fluffy kitten, but I never would have gotten away with a cat in the dorm. I suspected, correctly, that the girls would be somewhat less inclined to reveal the presence of a pet snake to the housemother for fear the thing would perhaps, somehow, appear under their pillow one night.

I also fancied Quetzalcoatl offered me some modicum of protection. You see, word had gotten out—I'm sure I don't know how—that the bite of *this* boa, unlike that of all others, was endowed with poison which, although mild, could prove fatal to some. I soon was given wide berth on my late night wanderings.

❀

The summer of 1970 found me desperately trying to put together a theater course I could take. I needed to add several extra credits required by the University of North Carolina, but I didn't want to stay in the States to get them. So, Mother and I went to the University of the Americas in Cholula, Puebla, a town of crumbling pyramids and 365 churches which was located at the foot of two awesome snowcapped volcanos.

The depressing saga of that summer (like my ballet fiasco of earlier days) is best left untold. Not unexpectedly, in light of my last college transfer, the theater courses offered in Cholula were suddenly cancelled due to technical difficulties beyond their control—the teacher quit.

The long and short of it is that at the end of the term, with the help of my parents and a wonderful lady soon dubbed "Mama" Clarine Furrow, I produced, directed, and starred in a public performance of *Miss Julie* in exchange for the needed credits. Considering most of the cast had either defected to go sightseeing or had gotten themselves arrested for various and sundry ridiculous reasons, the show was really not half-bad—except perhaps for the scene in which Daddy tried to create the illusion of "gaily dancing peasants" all by himself.

Finally the summer was over and I hadn't jumped into a volcano. My first night back in Chapel Hill, I hurried out to collect a small bouquet of leaves and flowers to give to Professor Koch. It was past midnight when I made my way to the theater and unlocked the doors. As usual, I slipped in quickly, locked the doors behind me and groped my way through the dark little lobby to the light switch at the entrance of the auditorium.

There was a soft click as pale lights flooded the stage.

"I'm back," I called out softly, "Professor Koch? I've come back...Here, I've brought you your flowers."

I placed the small bouquet on the stage. Silence.

"Professor?...Can you hear me? I've come back." The atmosphere began to swirl and thicken as though a great storm was about to break around me. "Professor...Professor...are you here?" I stood on the stage and looked out over the auditorium, my voice tense.

The inner swinging doors of the theater began to thud against the large front panels I had just locked, not the gentle sound which frequently announced the arrival of the professor, but violent, angry, threatening to shatter them into a thousand pieces. Then, as suddenly as it had begun, the banging stopped—dead silence—and then an overpowering presence of evil rushed into the theater and flooded around me. A voice—low, intense, quivering with rage spoke inside my head.

"Where were you? You left me. You've brought me no green thing to place upon my stage. Where were you?"

"Professor Koch...I'm sorry, I had to go away for the summer. Don't you remember, I came to say goodbye when I left? Why are you so angry?"

"You left me," the low voice hissed back, "You brought me nothing living, nothing green."

"I...I'm sorry, look...see, I've brought you flowers now. See? Here they are." I lifted the bouquet for him to see and placed it on the stage again.

"Leave me, I do not wish you with me now." It was the imperious voice of an angry lover, outraged by my neglect and in need of time to heal the wound.

"I'm sorry Professor Koch, I'm sorry." There were tears in my eyes, "May I come back later?" The only reply was a stony silence.

I left the theater confused and frightened.

For almost two weeks I visited the theater only in daylight. I took a daily offering of green things which I placed beneath the stage, and after a while I sensed he was no longer angry with me. And yet there was no longer that total acceptance of before. Now, sometimes when I would rise and go to the theater in the dead of night or in the early hours before dawn, I was greeted frequently by a barrier, invisible but as solid as though a web of rubber netting had been stretched across the entrance. I thought this was just temporary. Professor was still upset. He would get over it. Then several months later the final break came.

It was during the running of a comedy called *The Knack*. Kevan was stage manager for the play. I was busy with some obscure experimental show which was rehearsing at Graham Memorial. After my rehearsal I would walk over to Playmakers to watch the last act and help Kevan lock up the theater. Then we would sit by the stage and talk for a while before he would walk me home. Several nights into the performance, after everyone had left, Kevan flopped his long frame down into a seat in the front row and stretched his legs out on the ledge of the stage. "God, I'm exhausted," he sighed. "I can't wait for this show to be over."

"What's the matter, Kevan, didn't things go well tonight?" I asked him, sinking down into the seat on his right.

"Oh, no worse than usual. Guess I'm just tired."

"I don't blame you," I sighed. "This isn't exactly my favorite kind of comedy either, but at least you're working with a major production," I added wistfully.

"Yeah, I suppose so, but you wouldn't believe some of the silly things that have been going on backstage here." He was about to explain when something caught my eye to the left of the auditorium, behind him. I stared as Kevan continued speaking. His voice seemed to be coming from very far away. The form of a young soldier in a dark uniform began to materialize. He couldn't have been more than seventeen or eighteen years old. He was huddled on the floor by the wall, his whole body shaken by sobs that were now faintly audible to me. His head turned and he looked straight into my eyes, tears streaming down his face. He was clutching his right hip and suddenly I gasped in pain. Kevan stopped talking and looked at me. "What's the matter, Johanna?" His alarmed voice was still far away.

"Kevan, look." I said slowly.

Kevan followed my eyes to the point in the aisle where I was staring. "What are you talking about? Look at what?"

"Can't you see him, Kevan? There's a young soldier there. He's crying. I can feel the pain in my hip. Don't you see him?"

"...Ah, look Jo, I think it's time to go. Come on." Kevan stood up.

"But he's crying. He needs to say something to me."

"It's time to go, Johanna." Kevan's voice was firm. "I'm leaving now, are you coming?" Suddenly I felt afraid. I remembered Professor's anger towards me and didn't want to be in the theater alone tonight. I got up to leave. I looked again at the young soldier. As quickly as he had come, he began to fade, his face bitter, resentful, full of pain. He needed to speak and I had chosen not to stay. I had missed the moment. It was too late. "Yes...yes, let's go."

The next night I met Kevan backstage. "I won't be a minute, Jo," he said. "Just going downstairs to lock up. Want to come down with me?"

"No, you go ahead, I'll wait for you here." I was

hoping the young soldier would return. Kevan went below while I walked about the stage.

There was an old cot on the set and I stretched out on it to rest for a moment. I felt so tired. "I should have stayed last night to speak with him," I said to myself.

"Are you still here?" The auditorium grew suddenly cold as my eyes wandered across the seats to the lighting booth above. A tall pitch-black figure filled the booth. I whirled around on the cot as Kevan's footsteps came running up from beneath the stage. The figure faded and disappeared.

"Kevan! I think I saw someone in the light booth." I forced my voice to sound calm.

He gave me a strange look but went up to check. He waved and called down to me from the booth. "No one here." He was back a minute later. "Are you OK? You've been acting awfully strange lately. Are you sick?"

"No—No, I'm fine. Let's go get some coffee," I answered. But I felt cold and afraid. The figure had seemed hostile and threatening.

I went back again to the theater the following night though, determined not to be scared away. I went down front as usual to wait for Kevan.

The theater was ominously still. "I'm not going to let you get the better of me," I said softly as I stepped onto the stage. "This is as much my theater now as it is yours, Professor. I don't know if it's you trying to frighten me or if someone else has moved in, but it doesn't matter. I belong here too!" Intense vicious hatred rushed upon me, almost sucking the air from my lungs. Then, above me—a rustling sound. A dark hooded form—a hideous, contorted face, gleaming dead white, sprawled down on the grid over my head; enormous long eyes glinted bright shiny green—like the eyes of a wild maddened animal. Dark arms hung down—reaching for me.

I backed slowly to the wall fighting for breath, my mouth opened in a scream that would not come.

"Johanna! What's the matter?"

Kevan was standing before me. The pressure lifted and air rushed back into my lungs.

"Oh God, Kevan, there's someone up in the grid. I saw him."

"There's no one up there, Jo," his voice was openly exasperated. Just then we heard two footsteps on the iron walk-way above us.

"You're right! There *is* someone up there." He rushed up the ladder into the dimly lit walkway above the stage. I could hear the ringing of his footsteps as he searched the entire area; then he was back, his face white.

"Let's get out of here." He grabbed my arm and pulled me into the fresh night air.

Beck grinned as he saw us. "Hey, what timing!" he exclaimed as he crossed the street. "I was hoping I'd find you here."

"Beck, listen, weird things are happening in there. Jo's upset. Take her for some coffee will you? I've still got to lock up."

"Of course," Beck said, taking my arm. "Are you all right?" he asked me gently.

"Yes—yes…I'm fine now, Beck, thank you."

"I'll walk her home, Kevan," he said softly.

"Ah—yeah, OK. I've got some studying to do anyway. Good night Jo!"

"Good night."

Beck took my hand and guided me across the street. A car stopped to let us pass. I glanced up as we walked by and froze. The face in the car seemed to become the face I had just seen in the theater. I knew it couldn't be, but my nerves finally reached their snapping point as the car drove by. I began to scream. Beck held me a long time as I sobbed, terrified and helpless and broken hearted. Professor hated me. I no longer belonged.

Dear, gentle Beck. He seemed to be endowed with some sort of super human patience. At a time when I was most alone, most vulnerable, he stood by and helped me keep a grasp on sanity. He had been right; I needed him very much now.

Even Paula, my roommate, had moved out after leaving me a three page typed letter about how impossibly morbid, inconsiderate, theatrical, and bizarre I was. ("I would take you places with me more often if it weren't for the fact that I always have to *explain* you afterwards.") I'm sure she was right.

I never went into that theater again except to attend classes. I never again took Professor anything living and green.

❊

One night several weeks after the final incident in the theater, a number of us gathered in Jack and Adam's room to talk and listen to music. Beck and I were on some drug or other, a gentle kind of non-hallucinatory drug, the second of only four trips. I felt calm and mellow as I leaned back on his shoulder and waited for the music. We had been promised something different that night, a new rock musical on the life of Jesus called "Jesus Christ, Superstar." Rock was by no means a favorite of mine, but I was delighted with the songs even though it was obvious to me the composer's picture of a high-voiced, whimpy Jesus couldn't possibly be correct. Nevertheless, as the drug began to take effect, it seemed to me that I was suddenly *there,* an active participant in the drama of His life. *There* as He was betrayed. *There* as He was mocked, and oh, God, as He was beaten with a whip that seemed to cut into my own flesh with every crack.

There as His hands and feet were hammered to the cross. For the first time in my life I became acutely, overwhelmingly aware that Jesus had really lived, had really experienced death on a cross.

The first week I had been at Wesleyan, a girl named Nancy shared a little booklet called "The Four Spiritual Laws" with me and I had asked Jesus to become part of my life. For a few months afterwards things seemed better.

I always kept my Bible near and often read from the Book of Psalms to quiet my spirit when I felt myself surrounded by evil. I quickly found, however, that reading the New Testament seemed to precede an especially violent and frightening attack from the beings around me, so I began to avoid it. It was my love of God, however, that kept me from actively seeking to develop the psychic powers I knew I had. A voice deep inside me would say, "No, don't, it will hurt God if you do."

As the last strains of "Superstar" came to a close, I opened my eyes. I was alone. Everyone had left. I found Beck downstairs in the lounge. He had been unable to bear the pain of listening to the suffering of Jesus. We both decided we must find out more about this Man.

We began going to church early Sunday mornings. Several months later, we had an encounter with Deity.

We had been at what had inadvertently become an all-night theater troupe party. The music was mellow, the conversations deep, and no one wanted to go home. Mescaline, pot, and hash flowed freely through the group. Before dawn Beck and I asked a friend for a ride into town so we could attend the early chapel service. Our request elicited numerous moans and groans and comments of "I don't believe it!" But we got our ride and arrived in time. We sat in the dimly lit chapel, empty but for five or six women, and waited for the comforting, soothing words of the Anglican prayer book to be spoken.

With no warning, my heart began to pound and my eyes filled with tears. I felt suddenly as though the Eye of God, stern and awful, had broken through a cloud and was gazing down at me, at once loving and severe. "Why do you do this to yourself? Don't you know the harm you're bringing your spirit and body with those drugs?" The thought seemed to flow from the plain brass cross on the altar. "Don't you know I love you?" I hid my face in my hands and wept silently.

Later, as we walked down the grey, quiet street, Beck took my hand, "God doesn't want us to take drugs again, does He?"

I looked up surprised—"You felt it too?"

He nodded. "It's going to be hard."

He was right. It was hard.

But even though I still went to the evening gatherings of the Thespian clan, I never touched drugs again. My life-style, on the surface, changed dramatically.

An acid-head friend stole a copy of the Jerusalem Bible as a gift for us. We never did find out from where. Beck and I began to spend long hours reading it aloud to one another. Or, rather, Beck spent the hours reading it out loud to himself. I soon encouraged him to read instead from Tolkien's Ring Trilogy when we were together. Somehow I couldn't bear to hear the sound of the words from the New Testament for very long. The euphoria I had felt when listening to "Superstar" had become a black depression from which I could see no exit.

I no longer went to the theater, but I still frequented the graveyard and little chapel. Now hardly a night passed when dark figures did not wake me, softly whispering words in a language I couldn't understand, breathing their chill, foul breath on my face, pressing iron fingers across my arms and chest. As I walked at night trees became gruesome, grotesque shapes covered with evil eyes, watching, waiting...

Every time I crossed the street my heart pounded in terror for fear the demons would force some driver's hand to run me down.

Thoughts of death and intense rage filled my mind and I covered my journal with passages from Medea, The Bacchae, the Bad Seed, and the tortured poems of Edgar Allen Poe.

Half a dozen times I started up the hill to see one of the local psychiatrists—and as many times stopped part way up certain there was little they could do. The source of my problem wasn't psychological; it had its origin in a very different place, yet there was no one to whom I could turn to set me free. No one, perhaps, but God, and He seemed so far from me. My heart longed for Him, cried out for Him, but something barred my way. Weeping, I would fall to my knees. "My God, my God, why hast thou forsaken me? *why art thou* so far from helping me and from the words of my roaring? O my God, I cry in the daytime, but thou hearest not; and in the night season, and am not silent" (Psalm 22:1,2 KJV).

Then, at night, the evil beings would return and even my frantic whispering of the 23rd Psalm would not make them fade. Oh God, why couldn't I, as the Psalmist, fear no evil as I walked through the endless valley of the shadow of death. Why was there no comfort for me in His rod and staff?

And I would run to gentle Beck and he would hold me until my sobbing quieted. When in the winter of 1971 he asked me to marry him, I said yes.

9
Mind Control

The logs burned brightly in the enormous fireplace Mother had long since dubbed "Albert's Folly." Earlier that evening I had stood by hibiscus bushes in our lush garden watching the dark grey clouds gathering over the mountains. The breeze had been cool and refreshing. Now a gentle rain was falling on the Cuernavaca valley. The summer rains were beginning in earnest. I was curled on the sofa staring into the fire, absently watching the golden flames. A Brahms concerto played softly in the background and my little Siamese kitten, Solomon, purred, content and warm in my lap.

Mother sat in her blue velvet armchair, tagged "The Coffin Corner" by my Father in retaliation. She was reading an Agatha Christie mystery and smoking an ever present cigarette. From time to time I could sense her gaze on me, stern, concerned, loving. It had long been obvious to her I needed help; "psychiatric" was the category I knew to be under consideration. I couldn't say I blamed her. Agonizing recent scenes of my weeping and slamming my hand in fury against a wall leapt to my mind.

The last days in Chapel Hill had been a disaster. Mom and Dad had driven up to attend the graduation ceremonies, an event I deeply regretted at the time. Father had taken an instant, uncompromising dislike to Beck, an aversion he kept thinly disguised in reams of shredding sarcasm. Any young man presented as a future son-in-law would undoubtedly have received similar treatment. I was Papa's baby, his firstborn. No one was good enough for me, but especially not a soft-spoken, gentle, young, theater lighting technician who traveled with a makeshift theater troupe and sported long hair and a beard which, however kempt, shouted "hippie" at him. They couldn't see that Beck had probably saved my sanity, if not my life. Beck had cared enough to see me through one of the most difficult periods of my life. Even Damon was unable, or, understandably, unwilling to persevere through the maze in which I found myself. Beck had not demanded explanations I couldn't give or changes I was powerless to produce. I loved him for that. But I knew within weeks of my return to Mexico that a marriage could never work. I broke our engagement.

Father probably also, unfairly, blamed Beck for my involvement with drugs, such as it was.

"Kai had no right to tell them!" I thought to myself. Kai was a theater arts professor at Chapel Hill. He had known Mother when she did her graduate work there. "Only three people in this acting program have any real talent as far as I'm concerned," he once told me: "Damon, Malcolm and you." I treasured that—especially since having left Dr. Bryce I had received little encouragement and knew my work in theater, with but precious few exceptions, was abominable. Somehow Kai had found out I had occasionally been in on the theater pot-parties and felt obliged to tell Mother when he saw her that June at graduation. Intellectually I understood his motives, emotionally I felt betrayed. Well, Kai had no way of knowing I had stopped that

April anyhow. Now if only Mom and Dad would believe that. I had been so on edge, so depressed and moody, they were both certain I had to be on something. I sighed. They would never understand. Oh, God, if only I understood. I felt a constant, dark oppression all around me. Would I never be free of it?

The kitten shifted in my lap. I gently stroked his head.

"Hey, Johanna, listen to this," Father shouted up at me from his room where he was reading the newspaper, "and I quote: 'The Mind Control Method. In 48 hours you can learn to use your mind to do everything you wish. You can learn to overcome depression, relieve insomnia, eliminate negative thinking, avoid irrational fears, [Father's deep theater voice gave this last point special emphasis], relieve nervousness, develop ESP, and even gain peace of mind!' Sounds like something right up your alley, dear."

"What it sounds is bizarre," I said, coming into the room. "Probably some bunch of weirdos."

"More than likely, but at least it would give you something to do." He had a point there. There was not much for a "respectable" young American woman to do in Cuernavaca in those days. "They're having an introductory meeting tonight. Why don't you and Mother go check it out."

"On a Tuesday night in the rain?" I queried tentatively, not sure whether he was serious.

"So pretend it's Monday morning and take the umbrella," he retorted. We went.

The promises listed in the ad Father had seen were confirmed and embellished at the introductory meeting by a confident looking man in his mid-30's named Tom.

"You will indeed do many wonderful things by learning how to function at will at your Alpha brain wave," he said, "that level of mind tapped by the great geniuses, the great artists and masters, the great psychics. For example, I know of an old woman in Mexico City who performs astonishing healings and operations through having attained level 7, that is, control of the Delta frequency at which Cosmic Consciousness and Enlightenment are achieved. Now most of us here will probably never achieve such amazing control as this woman, Pachita, has, but you will be amazed nonetheless at what you will be able to do." Tom looked around the room at the fifteen or so people gathered and smiled broadly.

Then, using charts, he explained briefly about the primary brain frequency generated by the human mind as recorded by an Electroencephalograph (EEG). (The EEG is a very delicate and complex, not to mention expensive, electronic device used by scientists to detect brain waves.)

"The highest frequency is called Beta and is associated with the usual conscious state and functioning on the most basic five senses level. Reading a book or yelling at the dog who just messed up your carpet for the fourth time today is Beta activity." His audience chuckled at the joke and he steadied the chart he had almost knocked over with his pointer.

"Now the Alpha state," he continued, "is a lower, more stable frequency. Deep relaxation and meditation occurs at this level, as does regeneration of the body.

"The Theta and Delta states are even lower frequencies and are usually recorded during unconscious or deep sleep states.

"The whole purpose of Mind Control is to train people to gain control over the more stable Alpha brain waves to help them become superior human beings. The producing of phenomena not common to most of us at ordinary levels will be your final proof that you are indeed gaining mastery of your Alpha waves. I promise, each and every one of you who goes through the course will have ample proof of that on our last day.

"Let me make one thing clear: what we will be doing is not hypnosis—at no time will you relinquish control of your mind to anyone else. Rather, you will learn to tap into those deep levels of mind at will for any purpose you desire, as long as it is beneficial to yourself or mankind."

From what I could gather, Tom was implying that there was *nothing* a controlled mind could not do, from developing genius potential and overcoming bad habits to healing diseases and, literally, moving mountains. All that was needed for the mental and spiritual evolution of man was this 48-hour training program.

Tom bent over and pulled a new set of charts out from under the table. "Is everyone with me so far? Great! Let's go on then.

"The Mind Control training program is divided into four basic courses: The first one teaches Controlled Relaxation.

"In twelve hours you will learn how to relax at will and begin working in a state of mind that will heighten your creativity and efficiency. You will be able to sleep and awaken at will; to control and program your dreams to help you solve problems without stress and strain usually involved; to eliminate headaches, even migraines. How many of you here get migraines?" Several people raised their hands. "Well you don't have to anymore . . .unless, of course, you want to!

"The second course is called General Self-Improvement. It applies the principles of 'expanded levels of awareness' learned in the first course to specific problems. For example you'll learn techniques for eliminating habits such as smoking or overeating, improved memory and recall. You will learn to control physical pain and bleeding at will. Also, you'll be shown how to use a large mental screen (like a movie screen), to aid visualization and continue to expand your consciousness."

It certainly sounded worth a try. That next Saturday morning, June 26th, found Mother and myself stretched out side by side on the floor of a spacious but rustic living room, listening to an assertive voice read our "programming." Taped rounds of a metronome clicked and whirred monotonously providing a soothing background. I took a deep breath and relaxed.

I gave myself joyfully to these sessions, desperately clinging to everything Tom had to say as though they were the words of my salvation. I had returned to Mexico from Chapel Hill in despair and turmoil. I could see no hope—no light anywhere—no chance of ever breaking free from the forces which surrounded me. My copies of the King James Bible, *The Power of Positive Thinking,* and *The Power of Prayer* had done little to help. Here with Mind Control, however, was my salvation indeed. It *was* possible to gain control over unknown forces—to gain power and victory over them, and I thanked God for it. I let the phrases spoken by Tom during each session wash over me—"Every day in every way I am getting better, better, and better . . .I have full and complete dominion over my senses and faculties at this level of mind or at any other level, including the outer conscious level as this is so . . .I am always in control." Words of hope and freedom.

On the third day we began learning how to use visualization and image creation to help us develop our intuition and subjective communication—obscure terms used to describe ESP (which Tom called not Extrasensory Perception but, rather, Effective Sensory

Projection). We learned to project our minds into different metals, exploring the different textures and qualities of brass, lead and iron. We mentally traveled through a leaf, then a little animal—but gently—very gently. Little pet birds had been found suddenly dead after careless psychic handling. "It all might, at this stage, appear to be imaginary to some of you," Tom agreed, as a few members questioned the purpose of this section of the program, "but very real things are taking place on a different dimension. Trust me. It will all be proven to you on the last day. Meanwhile let's move on. You still need to create your laboratory before we're through for today."

This laboratory was a room of our own choosing which we created in our minds. It was to be our haven and refuge—our place for solving problems. It could look anyway we wanted; some chose French provincial, others early American. My room was a cave. The walls were made of amethyst and emerald crystals and glowed from within with a shimmering golden light. The gentle scent of roses and night jasmine permeated the room. There was a large royal blue velvet armchair which I placed in front of a fireplace, which was always kept lit. We were instructed to put two filing cabinets in the room; one for male problems, the other for female. My cabinets were made of the same material as the walls and stood within easy access of my chair. Next to them I placed a gracefully carved stand made of precious woods on which stood an alabaster vase filled with a golden ointment which I could use to help heal every wound and disease I was to encounter in the next year. Others created any number of tools, instruments, chemicals, medicines, and equipment they felt they might need. I opted for simplicity. To the right of the chair on the far side wall, we each installed a special compartment for transferring to and from different psychic levels. It had a special door which came down from the top and lowered into the floor.

Our laboratories now complete, we were ready to receive our counselors. We were told these counselors could be anyone we chose from Buddha to Grandma Moses, but we were not to be surprised by who actually showed up. They frequently were not the ones expected. (One rabbi taking a previous course had reportedly asked for Moses and Rebekah and wound up with a belly dancer and some pharaoh.)

There was no question at all in my mind whom I wanted for my counselors. There was no higher source of wisdom to whom I could appeal than Jesus. I wondered if it was a presumptuous request, but then remembered Jesus had said in the Bible: "Behold, I stand at the door, and knock: if any man hear my voice, and open the door, I will come in" (Revelation 3:20 KJV).

So I felt on that basis perhaps he wouldn't mind. Then, as we were told a female counselor was necessary, I decided upon Sarah Bernhardt. Having long since reached the conclusion I was not, after all, Sarah's reincarnation, I thought it might be nice to have her in residence. Perhaps she would bestow some much needed acting tips should I ever decide to go back into theater.

We were counted slowly down to our Alpha level by Tom and entered our now fully established laboratory. We each sat in our chair and by means of a control switch located on the arm, slowly brought down the special door of our special compartments to reveal—little by little—our counselors.

As my door came down, the room was filled with a radiant light that emanated from the figure standing behind it. Slowly, an inch at a time, the figure emerged. Shimmering brown hair parted in the middle, a high forehead, dark skin; eyes brown, deep and gentle. There! It was Jesus! The door went down now of its own accord, revealing the rest of the figure which was robed in a long white linen garment. He was glowing with a holy radiance and smiling softly. I stood, then fell at his feet.

Then Tom's voice instructed us to bring down our female counselor. I looked up. Again the door inched down this time to reveal an aged Sarah, curly red hair, wooden leg and all. I could hardly believe they had both deigned to come into my laboratory.

✳

That night I lay in bed thinking of all the wondrous things that had happened during the day. But perhaps I had imagined it—perhaps the Lord and Sarah were not actually my counselors. I would go down to my psychic laboratory and call them again. Yes, I knew Tom had warned us against doing that, but I had to know if I had the right ones. It was too important.

I slowly stretched my body and nestled into my pillows as I began to count down to Alpha. Once in my laboratory, I sat in my chair and surveyed the crystals that shone with the richness of Tiffany stained glass. It was so beautiful there. I turned my chair to face the door. "Oh, Lord," I prayed, "please, reveal the counselors I'm truly meant to have." The chamber door began lowering—the same radiance shining from behind it—but something was wrong . . .The hair was wild and matted, the forehead was covered with a coarse fur and the eyes were slanted, gleaming and wild—like the eyes I had seen in Playmakers Theater. Fresh blood smeared the muzzle and oozed down long white fangs; the droplets spattered down the front of the tunic. Yet the rest of the figure was the same as before, covered in a long linen robe and gleaming. The figure stood growling, snarling softly as he watched me. A numbing cold paralyzed my body on the bed.

"Oh, God—let me out—let me out!" my mind screamed, but I wasn't able to come out of level. Minutes (hours?) of suffocating horror. Then, suddenly, through sheer force of will, something snapped and I felt myself hurtled from my laboratory. My body shot upright. My whole system was in shock. I was trembling. I thought visitations like this were over . . .but I had disobeyed instructions. I brought this thing upon myself. "God, forgive me! Help me!" I turned on the light by my bed. Perhaps my rashness would not be held against me. Surely in the morning everything would be all right.

❊

The fourth and final day of our Mind Control Training was tagged "Applied ESP" and had long been heralded as the "final proof" day. Today we would know for certain we were indeed functioning at Alpha and received true psychic information.

Tom handed out sheets explaining basic human anatomy. "Today is the day we've been waiting for," he smiled at us. "We'll begin by helping you establish, at Alpha level, points of reference within the human body so that ultimately you will be able to detect, and correct, any abnormalities sensed within the organism. In fact, by the end of the day, you'll be 'reading cases' much as the famed psychic Edgar Cayce did, with the difference that Cayce *lost* consciousness at his deeper levels. You'll be performing similar feats at a deep though conscious level of mind, and will not lose control as he did. Go ahead and find a comfortable position on the floor and let's begin."

During the first programming session of that day we counted ourselves down to level. We were told to enter our laboratories and greet our counselors. I felt afraid as we went down, but tried to relax as the monotonous sound of the metronome began. Surely everything would be fine.

Two figures were in the lab waiting for me, facing the wall. They turned slowly towards me as I entered—I gasped. Both Sarah and Jesus now had werewolf faces. They just stood there watching me, growling softly. I suddenly understood they were not going away; I was going to have to deal with them face to face. After a long moment I gathered courage and approached the two figures. As I did they began changing. The face of Jesus flashed on—shining and loving—then in a flash, the werewolf reappeared. The same was happening with Sarah—on and off—on and off. I forced myself to approach the figure of Jesus and said, "Lord, why are you and Sarah doing this? It frightens me." Jesus' face appeared, smiling and gently.

"Do not be afraid," he said., "We only want to teach you that not everything that seems to be evil on the surface really is evil down beneath in its essence. When you truly understand this, our werewolf faces will be gone forever and you will ever see us as we really are."

The words sounded in my mind as clearly as though they had been spoken aloud, but they made no sense to me. Then suddenly it was clear: however frightening these beings appeared, they were not evil. I decided to learn to trust and accept them regardless of the discrepant images they might present. It seemed as though it was all designed to strengthen me and make me grow in spiritual understanding.

The evil faces reappeared, grinning hideously—waiting for my response to their revelation.

"I accept what you have told me. I will try to learn my lesson soon, Lord." I approached him and he bent to receive my kiss upon his woolly blood matted forehead.

"Thank you, little one," came a gentle voice.

Tom had counted us up several minutes before, but I hadn't heard him. When I finally opened my eyes I realized everyone else was up and around and looking at me oddly. It was several weeks before I was able to gain enough control of my fear of the beings to warrant the disappearance of the werewolf faces.

About a month later I went through the course a third time. Kim took it with me at the Mexico City house. She also asked for Jesus as her counselor as she had been a commited believer for several years. She had been reluctant to take the course but did so at our urging. When time came to receive her counselors, she said the face of Satan pressed in on her; then, a loud crash and a powerful voice cried out, "Thou shalt have no other gods before me!" as the satanic vision vanished. She was convinced she had seen Satan and that Mind Control was occultic and spiritually dangerous. Because of what my counselors had told me, however, I decided she simply had not evolved sufficiently to understand what had really happened. Why had she been so afraid? After all, I had seen my horrors and faced them head on. That seemed the only way to handle the situation. No true spiritual progress could be made by running away from what was fearful. It had to be dealt with face to face. "Too narrow minded," I concluded. "She'll never truly grow spiritually." So I discounted all her frantic warnings.

❀

As Tom had promised, that last day of Mind Control was a tremendous success. We did indeed receive all the proof we needed of our working at Alpha. We had each been asked to bring several three by five cards, each with the name, age, sex and geographic location of some individual personally known to us—preferably someone with a serious illness or disability of some sort. As complete a composite as possible of that person's condition was to be made and written on the card, which was then turned in to Tom without being shown to anyone else. He distributed the cards at random—two or three per person. We then divided into groups of three—preferably not with close friends, and went off to find a secluded place to work. One person was to act as the psychic, another as the orientologist who would help guide the beginning psychic in his exploration. A special orientologist's sheet was provided for this purpose. The third person was to function as a secretary, writing down what the psychic said for documentation. Each person would "read" several cases and then switch roles.

The psychic was directed to enter his laboratory, greet his counselors and say his welcome prayer (which could range anywhere from "Hi, glad you're here" to the Lord's Prayer). Then the orientologist helped count the psychic down to an even deeper level of mind where he was told he would be accurate and correct in the reading. "At the count of three, the body of *name, age, address, sex,* will be on your screen —one, two, three (snap of fingers)—the body of *name, age, address, sex* is on your screen. Sense it, feel it, visualize it, imagine it, create it, know it is there—take it for granted it is there. Scan the body with your intelligence from where you know is the head to where you know are the feet—up and down, up and down—once a second. While scanning the body in this manner allow your intelligence to indirectly select three areas of greatest attraction."

These areas were then mentioned as the psychic perceived them. He was encouraged to say whatever came to his mind. The areas of attraction were then amplified and the possibilities of afflictions or malfunctions were allowed to enter the psychic's mind. "Keep talking as you investigate, tell me everything that you are inclined to say. You will feel as though you're making it up. This is the right feeling. Tell me all your impressions whether you think they are right or wrong." Where the psychic was accurate, he was told to review his feelings at that point to make it easier to recognize his accuracy on other readings. The counselors often gave the information needed and, occasionally, even in medical terms unknown to the psychic. Frequently not all the information had been included on the card and something sensed by the psychic would be greeted with exclamations of surprise when discussing the case with the person who submitted the card (who, incidentally was not to be in the room during the reading) saying they had forgotten all about that particular condition. Frequently the person who submitted the card would later learn the person did indeed have or had some ailment or condition the other person was not even aware of (such as scars or broken bones).

Some thought perhaps our results in the readings were merely extraordinarily fortunate bits of guesswork. To prove the point, the skeptics were instructed to attempt reading a case without first going to Alpha level. They failed dismally. Given the vast range of possible diseases, malfunctions, and conditions of the human body, accurate *guesswork* was out of the question. We were indeed perceiving information psychically. The theory behind all this activity was that if information could be *picked up,* then information could also be *transmitted*, whether the person on the receiving end was aware of it or not. If so, then diseases could be reversed and healed (sometimes the psychic would "operate" on the tumor, or "crush" kidney stones with a metal hammer or "rub" a healing balm on aching joints). Problems could be solved; disasters could be foreseen and prevented.

To avoid a slew of self-proclaimed doctors from

flinging themselves on society at large, Tom emphasized that we were " . . .never to diagnose. Only medical people have license to diagnose and heal. We conduct psychic investigation and detect abnormalities and malfunctions at psychic level." At the end of each reading the orientologist would say, "Every time you enter this dimension with the sincere desire to help humanity, you will be helping yourself. Your talents will increase and you will become more accurate every time. And this is so." Our aim was to be the good of humanity. I don't think there was one of us there that day who was not awed at the possibilities and the power now within our grasp. We had been taught all the basics. Now it was only a matter of practice.

And practice I did, consciously keeping myself at Alpha as long as possible during my waking hours and programming my sleep at night to remember and interpret dreams. I read as many cases as I could on my own, or with a friend named Joan* who recorded my increasing accuracy. As was the case with other Mind Control graduates, I was perceiving not only physical problems but spiritual and psychological difficulties as well, frequently gaining information on their pasts as well as their futures.

I was also beginning to practice psychometry, that is, seeking information from sensing the vibrations of an object.

On the evening of July 15th, 1971 a small group of us met for dinner at the Jensen's*. Like so many people in Mexico, the Jensens were avid collectors of artifacts. After dinner they took us on a tour of their artifact room. It was filled with all manner of wonderful masks, statues, and objects collected over the years from all over the world, though primarily from Mexico. Mr. Jensen paused at one table which displayed part of his African collection. He picked up a bracelet. It was a strange object made of intertwining metals that looked like brass and silver. He said nothing as he handed it to Tom, but merely asked him whether he could perceive anything about it at level. We all sat on the veranda while Tom went down to level.

As he was concentrating, I was startled to see the shadowy figure of an Arab dressed in long white robes standing just behind Tom's right shoulder. He was staring down at the bracelet, his eyes riveted on the object. I almost cried out but then realized Tom was not in danger. I kept silent and watched. The figure drew back into the garden; I could see him by a tree. Two natives, tall and handsome and gleaming as though oil had been rubbed into the skin, appeared by the wall to Tom's right. The woman wore little besides an elaborate loin cloth, some gold chain necklaces and earrings. The bracelet Tom was holding was on her left wrist. They just stood there staring. Several minutes passed. Tom came up from level shaking his head. He could see nothing about the bracelet. I told them of the beings who were standing there and asked for the bracelet.

As I counted down, I felt suddenly transported to a strange country. I was standing at the edge of a gorge; the countryside was rocky, dry and bushy. Far below was a river, angry and swollen from rains far upstream. Across the gorge I could see the Arab who had been behind Tom. Another man was with him. They were arguing violently over several small chests filled with jewelry. Then I saw the Arab push the man over the cliff. I could hear him screaming as he fell. The Arab hastily replaced the objects which had spilled from one of the chests during the scuffle; several pieces hidden by a small shrub were inadvertently left behind. That was all I could see. It all seemed to happen in an instant and then was over. I opened my eyes and put the bracelet down. I couldn't hold it any longer. As I told the group what I had seen, Mr. Jensen looked excited. It was impossible to confirm what I had seen, but the man who had given the bracelet to him had found it in a location very like the one I described.

❀

It was during the days of July 13-16, when I was going through the Mind Control course for the second time, that the wonderful visions began. One morning as I went into my laboratory, I immediately felt myself strangely light—almost weightless. My counselor Jesus was standing there—waiting for me. I saw myself floating towards him—drawn by him. The intense golden glow emanating from him was almost blinding. It filled the entire room, absorbing into the crystal walls which then gave back the golden rays. He was smiling at me. It had been almost a week since I had last seen the werewolf faces, and I was beginning to conquer my fear. His right hand was filled with a liquid fire; the flames flickered and danced as he cupped it in his hand. As I stood before him, he poured the fire over my head. It grew and flowed over my body until I was engulfed by it. It was cold yet burned and a strange sweet odor filled the room. Soft voices surrounded me with wonderful sounds of music. Then I saw a woman, beautiful with flowing hair and robes of shimmering dark blue spangled with tiny stars. I could see her dimly at first as she appeared through the translucent crystals. She came towards me. She took me by the shoulders and gently kissed me on the forehead. The third finger of her right hand pressed between my eyebrows, just to the right. "Welcome, my child." Then she turned and floated back through the wall as she had come. I have never experienced such joy, such light and peace, such unspeakable ecstacy. I was on the right path at last.

On the 22nd of July, during my third consecutive run in the program, Sarah, who had never said a word to me during the twenty-five days she had been with me, stood up and announced it was time for her to leave; she had been with me as long as she could spare and was needed elsewhere. The time had come for me to receive a new counselor. With that, she turned and left the room.

Seconds later, a small Mexican Indian woman materialized. She didn't arrive as the other two had. It was her eyes that held me. Everything seemed to form around them. They were penetrating eyes, a deep amber in color; the eyes of one with ageless wisdom for whom there were no longer any surprises. Her face was chiseled; wrinkled, but still beautiful. Long grey hair was braided and tied in a loop behind her back. She wore a simple ankle-length blue cotton dress, a maid's full apron and simple sandals. Despite her aristocratic face, her whole appearance was that of a servant. As she appeared, that is the word that came to me: "Servant."

I immediately assumed she was Pachita, but when I described her to Tom, he shook his head. Whoever I had seen, it was not Pachita. He suggested I ask her who she was, which I did.

"Will you tell me who you are? I mistook you for Pachita. Forgive me." A faint smile crossed the woman's face.

"You gave me no chance to tell you who I am," she said. "You are to call me *Mamacita*. (Little Mother). I have come to remind you of your coming role as servant. I will teach you humility and lead you into true wisdom."

"I am honored you have come, Mamacita. I am willing to learn all you have to teach me," I answered, overwhelmed at her presence. I knew with her arrival that the time had come for me to meet Pachita.

10
The Beautiful Side of Evil

The six days following my first meeting recounted earlier with Pachita were spent in deep mental and spiritual preparation. I sensed I was on the brink of my life's work and ultimate fulfillment in my search for God. I knew the years of fear were over; my spirit guides, Jesus and Mamacita, were with me, teaching me to overcome the lower spiritual entities. Now, during the many hours spent in meditation waves of light and peace would flow over me, pushing away the darkness.

On Friday July 27, 1971, the morning of the seventh day, I returned to see Pachita. Father Humberto and Peggie* asked to go with me. Padre Humberto, a Catholic priest and movie actor, had broken his leg in a car accident and was living at the Mind Control house in Cuernavaca while he recovered. I don't think he had met Pachita before. He hoped *Hermanito Cuauhtemoc* (that is, "Little Brother," as the spirit who worked through Pachita was affectionately called) would heal his leg so he could return to the work he was doing with lepers in a colony near Tepoztlan.

Peggie, who was also living at the Mind Control house, had an operation at Pachita's about five weeks before. Hermanito had begun plugging the holes in her skull, which was decalcifying. He had also removed an inoperable brain tumor. The red scar was clearly visible on the back of her head when she pulled her hair apart to show me.

Daddy decided to join us that day. He was profoundly skeptical of the things he had heard about Pachita, but was wearing his "I'm determined-to-be-open-minded-about-this" look, so I was hopeful he would eventually accept her.

We arrived at Pachita's around 11:30 in the morning. The courtyard was already crowded with people waiting to see Hermanito. Many had been there since before dawn. Several women were organizing the crowd in preparation for Hermanito's arrival: married women and their children were to be seen first, then the men, and last of all the unmarried women. Entrance coupons were sold for ten pesos each (about eighty American cents at the time). Young children and the very poor were not charged. I later learned this fee was a recent innovation devised by her assistants to help support Pachita, whose failing health no longer allowed her to go out on the streets selling trinkets and lottery tickets. She herself had never charged for the healings.

Each person in line was instructed to have a fresh raw egg to present to Hermanito for the spiritual *limpia* (cleansing) which was performed on everyone during the morning consultation sessions. I had forgotten our eggs and hurried out with several others in the line to purchase them at the market across the street. I handed Daddy, Peggie and Padre Humberto their eggs, then took my place in line to wait.

When my turn finally came, I entered the dark little anteroom still guarded by falcon Ursula and waited behind the plastic curtain with one of the assistants who monitored the flow of people into the altar room. I could feel powerful vibrations emanating from that room and started to pull the curtain aside to see what was happening, but the woman quickly stopped me.

"No!" she whispered. "Keep it shut until the patient in there leaves! The curtain is here to keep any 'evil airs' that person may have brought with him from attacking you."

"I see," I mumbled apologetically.

"Is this your first consultation with Hermanito?" Her voice softened. I nodded.

"Then be sure you remember not to address him as 'Pachita.' It is her body you will see, but she is not in it."

I nodded again. Tom had explained that to me before. Pachita was always addressed in the masculine and as "Hermanito" when the spirit was present.

Minutes later the woman pulled aside the plastic curtain for me and I stepped in.

Pachita was standing near the altar. She was wearing a short sleeved cotton dress covered by a dirty yellow satin garment that was tied in a knot at the shoulder. It was decorated with sparkles glued on in geometric designs and was worn by Pachita whenever Hermanito Cuauhtemoc was holding consultation sessions or operations. Pachita's eyes were tightly shut, one of the signs that Pachita herself, her spirit, was no longer there. Yet it was as though she saw clearly. I was later to watch her deftly thread a needle even though her eyes could not possibly have seen to do so.

There were three other assistants in the room—an old Mexican woman who stood to Pachita's right and held a plastic bottle filled with a sweet smelling balsam; then a young man, an engineer and Yaqui Indian whom I later came to know as "Chalio," acted as secretary writing down any prescriptions or medications prescribed. The third person stood by the exit door to usher people out when their time with Hermanito was over.

I stood before Hermanito, still holding the egg in my hand. He placed both hands on my shoulders and, in a voice much deeper and gruffer than Pachita's own, commanded, *"A trabajar, m'hijita"* ("To work, my little daughter.") A strange shock ran through my body as his hands touched me.

"How do I begin, Hermanito?" I asked as he took the egg and began rubbing it briskly over my head and shoulders. He tossed the egg at the bucket that stood near him. It splattered on the floor. Hermanito nodded towards Memo, Pachita's oldest son, who was sitting on the cot.

"The son of my flesh will give you instructions (Hermanito always spoke of Pachita in the third person calling her *"mi carne"* or "my flesh.") He cupped his right hand towards the woman standing by him who filled it with the sweet smelling balsam with which all who came before him were anointed. He rubbed it between his palms, then placed both hands firmly upon my head as he murmured something I could not understand. Then he brushed his hands down my body as though whisking lint off my clothing, front and back. Again his hands grasped my shoulders and the sightless eyes peered into my own. *"A trabajar!"*

Memo stepped outside with me as I left.

"What did Hermanito mean, Memo?" I asked him. Memo looked at me oddly.

"Hermanito is telling you that you will work as a full trance medium—that you will one day heal as my mother does. You are to begin preparing immediately. Come back this Monday. Hermanito himself will tell you what you must do."

Padre Humberto had also been told to return on

Monday. Hermanito had promised to give him a cure for leprosy. As for Papa, his reception was cool. Hermanito seemed to have a kind of X-ray vision and could diagnose the exact disease or discomfort of the person before him without having been given a clue. It was odd then that he should have asked Father what the matter was. Papa was not well at all at the time, but to test Hermanito had answered, "Oh, nothing. I'm fine."

"Why in that case," Hermanito said with excessive politeness, "this house is at your service when required."

❋

Several weeks later, Padre Humberto and I waited in Pachita's living room for hours. We had been told to be there at noon. It was now six o'clock in the evening and still Pachita was not there. A small television set, a gift from a grateful American patient, had been blaring forth some highly obnoxious soap operas all afternoon. Pachita's daughter wanted to hear it in her bedroom. I spent the time recording the events of the last several weeks in my diary and feeding bits of meat to Ursula. It was beginning to get dark and thunderclouds were thick and grey. "It's going to be pouring on the way home," I thought dismally as I walked back to the living room. The mountain pass between Mexico City and Cuernavaca could be treacherous anytime, but especially so in the rain.

At 6:15 Memo and Pachita arrived. Memo threw me a dark look as he walked by. He nodded curtly but said nothing. Pachita went into the kitchen to have supper. As always, a group of people had gathered to see Hermanito. One was a rather large girl who had a bandage wrapped around her neck. Her mother told me the girl had been the victim of a curse. A year or so before she had become very ill, but none of the many doctors she had seen had been able to give a diagnosis. Finally they found their way to Pachita through a friend. A week ago Hermanito had operated on her, materializing and removing a very large tarantula from her throat. The thing was to be kept in a box for a specified period of time, but had somehow escaped. The mother was worried perhaps the girl might need another removal of the curse. I learned later that she did not.

After her supper Pachita entered the altar room. We were told Hermanito would give only *consultas* (consultations) that night. There were to be no operations. There was an exclamation of dismay from a woman who had been waiting patiently for several hours.

"Oh, please, Hermanito told me last week he would operate on me tonight. My cataract operation at the hospital is scheduled in four days—Please let Hermanito operate on me tonight!"

"Well," said Pachita shrugging her shoulders, "it is up to Hermanito. We will ask him during the *consultas* and see what he says."

Pachita lumbered across the courtyard and into the altar room with three of her associates. One by one the people who needed to see Hermanito filed in. I was about to go in myself when Pachita came out. She patted Rita* on the shoulder. "Prepare yourself. Hermanito will operate tonight after all."

Several minutes later Amado, a man who had been with Pachita for over eleven years, asked Rita to enter the altar room. "Only three other people will be allowed to enter to witness the operation," he announced. Her husband, Alex*, was immediately by her side. Padre Humberto went in as did another man who had been there several times before. Pachita looked at me as she walked by.

"You too, little daughter—Come along."

It was beginning to rain. The sound of the large drops was magnified as they pelted the tin roof of the altar room. Water was beginning to seep under the door and onto the coarse cement floor. Everything seemed drained of color, reflecting rather the flat grey of the thunderclouds above us. A candle was lit and placed upon the altar. The single naked light bulb was switched off. Pachita put on Hermanito's satin robe and sat on the straight-back wooden chair in front of the altar. She told us to gather around her and pray. The scrawny woman stood at Pachita's side holding the ever present bottle of protective holy balsam. She poured some into Pachita's hands and began a low chanting prayer which she muttered almost inaudibly as Pachita rubbed the balsam over her hands, into her hair and down the front of her body. She closed her eyes, placed her hands straight and stiff on her spread knees, and began taking deep breaths. The atmosphere in the room seemed to thicken as a powerful unseen presence descended upon Pachita. Suddenly her body quivered violently. Her right hand raised in a sharp straight-armed salute and a deeper, stronger voice than hers announced *"Estoy con ustedes, hermanos queridos"* ("I am with you, beloved brothers"). Pachita had vacated the shell of her body to make way for Hermanito.

Hermanito arose and directed Rita to sit in the chair. Rita, obviously nervous, did so.

"Keep praying, my little ones," Hermanito said to us. "Only with God's will and help will we be able to heal this woman's eye." Chalio stood behind Rita on Hermanito's left side. He had cut large strips of cotton from the roll Alex had brought. Smaller patches were placed in a small bowl and alcohol was poured over them, Hermanito's one concession to physical antiseptics. Alex had been standing beside by his wife, but now he turned away and sat on the cot, head in his hands. He had helped in a number of operations in the past but he chose to pray during this one. Hermanito called me to his side.

"Come, little daughter, you will help me." He instructed me to hold a large block of cotton under Rita's chin.

"Rita," Hermanito said, "I want you to sit very still now. Keep your eyes open and looking up at the ceiling. Do you understand me, little one?"

"Is it going to hurt me, Hermanito?" she asked, her voice quivering as she spoke.

"No, little one, you are even now being anesthetized," Hermanito said reassuringly as he stroked her hair. He took the new bottle of alcohol I was holding, opened it and poured it directly into her eye. I gasped, expecting the woman to cry out, but she just sat there. Then Hermanito sprinkled some of the balsam on the eye.

"Very well, little one, now hand me the cotton you have there." As I handed him the smaller cotton strips, he formed a square leaving the eye exposed in the center. He had stepped behind Rita and to her left. I moved directly in front of her, my knees brushing against hers. Then he asked Amado for the scissors and the old knife that lay on the altar. Amado quickly wiped each with a square of cotton soaked in balsam and handed the scissors to him. Hermanito took the scissors and raised them in a salute toward the altar as he began a prayer in *Nahuatl,* the ancient Aztec language. His first words were audible, then died down to a whisper. As he prayed, I saw that the area where we stood, and especially around Rita's head, became much brighter than the rest of the room, as though a soft spotlight were shining down on us. I could see clearly. I was to witness this phenomenon at each of the several hundred operations in which I assisted in the coming months.

"Pray to God, little ones!" Hermanito pushed one point of the scissors into Rita's eye and began to cut. A pale reddish-white liquid trinkled into a piece of cotton that fell off her face and dropped onto her chest. I caught it and replaced it, my face only inches from her eye.

"Do you feel pain, little one?" he asked her.

"No, Hermanito," Rita answered. Her head began to turn as she spoke.

"Keep your eyes open—*open*." He took the knife from Amado, raised it in a salute, then began peeling a thin opaque scum off the center of the eye. It broke. He placed the first piece on the cotton I held out, then he gently lifted off the second part of the tissue and handed it to me. Again he poured alcohol into the eye, then placed a clean pad of cotton over it.

"We have finished, dear brother," he said to Chalio. "You may bandage the eye now."

When the job of bandaging was done to his satisfaction, he instructed two men to wrap Rita in a sheet and carry her across the courtyard to rest in the house.

"Keep her lying down for one hour—head back. Then give her some red herb tea to drink. You'll find it in the kitchen." Alex was instructed to keep her quiet for three days, after which the bandage could be removed. The entire procedure had taken perhaps fifteen minutes. Chalio handed Hermanito a large piece of cotton soaked in balsam with which to cleanse his hands. A week later I learned that Rita's operation at the hospital had been cancelled. The doctors were astonished at the total disappearance of the cataract.

The room became darker now. I became aware again of the rain which was now pounding violently on the tin roof. The water on the floor where I stood was about half an inch deep.

As Rita was carried out, Hermanito sat down on the chair—legs spread, hands on his knees. Padre Humberto approached him. I saw Hermanito take his hand and pat it warmly as he smiled. I had moved out of the way to the back of the room and couldn't hear what was said. Padre Humberto later told me Hermanito had instructed him to continue his mission to the lepers and gave him a recipe based on the juice of ground buzzards which would cure leprosy and certain forms of cancer. Then Padre turned to me and called me to them. Hermanito took my hand.

"This is the girl who will help you with your lepers. She is ready now to work as a full medium. In three weeks another spirit whom I have sent and even now is with her will begin to work through her." (I thought of Mamacita.) Hermanito then told us that for three weeks, either on a Thursday or a Monday, Padre and I were to meet either at two o'clock in the afternoon or at eight o'clock in the evening.

"You are both to pray. You, my little daughter, watch me closely. You're to sit in a straight chair with your hands in your lap, thus, even as you saw my flesh earlier this evening. Relax and breathe deeply. Go down to level as you have learned. Then do this with your hands." (Here he showed a special circular movement of the hands). "Then place your hands again on your lap and wait. Padre, when you see her hands begin to shake and rise from her lap, you are to place your own hands over hers and say 'I give you the light of the Lord. May the light of the Lord be with you.' Pray continually that no evil overtake her. May the Lord go with you, little ones."

❋

That Thursday, Padre Humberto and I met as Hermanito had ordained.

"Almighty God," I prayed before we began, "more than anything else You know I love You and want to serve You. Help me now become an instrument of Your hand. I give myself to You, O Lord. Guide us now in this work. Help us discern what is false and of our imagination from what is of You. Protect us from any evil being who would hinder this work which You have set before me. Let your perfect will be done, Holy God." I performed the motion with my hands, then breathed deeply and relaxed.

Almost immediately I felt myself encircled by a golden glow. My hands began to feel very, very light and detached from the rest of my body and began to rise. From far away I heard Padre's voice: "I give you the light of the Lord. May the light of the Lord be with you." I was surrounded by a large number of people who stood in a circle around me—shadowy unknown figures which were touched with the golden glow that now had expanded to include them. Pachita's spirit, more solid than the rest, stood before me; Cuauhtemoc, towering just behind her, his figure almost merging with her own. Mamacita, my Indian counselor, stood by her. Then I saw my counselor Jesus, translucent, shimmering with a glow brighter than all the rest. My spirit stood and I approached him with my hands outstretched. Again a flame of purification was in his hand. He poured the flames into my hands. They burned and yet were cold, and I was filled with joy and peace. It seemed that the Lord had heard my prayers and had sanctified my hands to his use.

The second week the feeling during our session was quite different. I saw two giant golden doors which slowly swung open—then shut again before I could pass through them. The figures which had surrounded me the week before stood on the other side beside a large book which lay open on an invisible stand. I knew that the mysteries of life were contained within its pages. Suddenly, the doors swung open and did not shut. I walked through and stood before the book. A towering figure, like an angel in its flowing robes, stood behind it. He placed it in my hands, but I knew the time had not yet come to read from it. I knew many sorrows, many trials, must be faced and overcome before I would be worthy to read and understand.

"Oh, God," my spirit prayed, "grant me the courage, faith, and perseverance to obey Your will."

❃

After that session with Padre Humberto, I drove into Mexico City as often as I could to be at Pachita's. That Monday and Tuesday I was asked to stand at the curtain at the entrance of the altar room. Tom told me to be sure to be at the Mind Control house rather than at Pachita's on Wednesday, however. Hermanito had promised to operate on a 72-year-old man who had flown in from Los Angeles to see him.

A large group of Mind Control people gathered to witness the event, but the hours dragged on and still Pachita did not arrive. We assumed perhaps Hermanito had operated that night at her home after all, and that she would arrive later, but by midnight still no word had come. There was no phone at Pachita's as yet, so several of us decided to drive the forty minutes to her house to see what had happened. There was a light on when we arrived, so we knocked. Enrique, one of her sons, opened the gate.

"Sorry you can't see her, everyone has just gone to bed," he said.

"No, wait. I'm up," Pachita called from the living room. "I'm sorry I couldn't come. The government people have been here all day. Seems they think I'm practicing medicine without a license." She smiled broadly. "What do they know, the fools. Anyway, we raised enough to pay them off. They won't be back for a while." She waved a hand at me, "Come, little one, help me get my things. I will come with you."

We walked into the altar room. She handed me various things to put into a large empty bag for her: Hermanito's cloak, the balsam, some hospital kidney bowls, a new bottle of alcohol, and a jar which contained two vertebrae.

"My friend in the morgue got these for me this morning—a poor man was run over last night." Then she handed me Hermanito's knife, which I also placed in the bag. (Human parts were not always used in the operations. It was not any more necessary than the use of anesthesia or antiseptics.)

When we returned to the house, Mr. Smith* and his wife were awakened and told to prepare. Pachita had a quick cup of coffee, then went in to examine him. She prodded and pushed on his back, asking where it hurt. Then she took a small clean glass which I brought from the kitchen. At her request I lit a match and briefly held it to the mouth of the glass. There was a small exploding sound within the glass as she quickly pressed the rim down into the small of his back. The skin began to bulge and rise, becoming a dark purple as it grew. Pachita nodded to herself.

"Move him to the floor now." A large, clear plastic sheet had been made ready at the foot of the bed. Mr. Smith stretched face down upon it. A large candle was lit and placed on a bureau near him. Many of the Mind Control group who had been there earlier that evening had reassembled and now crowded into the room to watch; a rare event, for usually only a few witnesses were allowed. Meanwhile, after a pair of scissors had finally been located, Pachita had me cut strips of cotton from a new roll. Some of the strips were placed in the little kidney bowls and soaked with alcohol, others were soaked in the balsam, while still others were kept dry. Pachita put on her robe, rubbed the balsam over her hair and clothes, and sat in a straight chair to await Hermanito.

After a few moments she shuddered and her arm raised in the now familiar salute. "I am with you, my little ones." Pachita's eyes were tightly shut. Hermanito motioned to me.

"Come, my daughter; you will assist me tonight." We knelt by Mr. Smith. I was on Hermanito's left.

"Someone go and talk to the man during the operation and translate to him for me. Hold his hand—Keep him talking—I don't want him to lose consciousness." One of the women knelt by Mr. Smith's head and began speaking softly to him. Hermanito had me pull up Mr. Smith's pajama top and fold his waistband down just enough to expose the lower back. I handed him a piece of alcohol-soaked cotton, which he rubbed briskly over the old man's back. Four large pieces of dry cotton were arranged in a square, leaving the spinal area where he would operate uncovered. He took the scissors in his hand and looked up at the intense faces in the room.

"Lift your thoughts to God, my little ones—pray!"

"Ask him if he is in pain." No he wasn't. Hermanito plunged one end of the scissors into his back. Mr. Smith groaned as it penetrated his skin. I saw the scissors disappear into the back. I heard the flesh being cut. My hands on either side of the wound felt a warm thick liquid flow into the cotton. Mr. Smith groaned again.

"Keep him talking—is he feeling pain? Ask him!"

Yes, some, but he could bear it. Hermanito pulled the scissors out. He took his knife, raised it in supplication and pushed it into Mr. Smith's back. I felt a fresh surge of warm liquid ooze up from the wound and over my fingers on the cotton. Hermanito cut away for several minutes, then reached in and pulled out what seemed to be an odd-shaped bone covered with blood and bits of red flesh.

"This is one of the vertebrae, little one. It is badly damaged." Hermanito then took a bone from the jar. As he did, I looked down into the dark gaping wound in Mr. Smith's back and felt a moment of panic.

"My God, how will this ever close and be whole again!" But then Hermanito turned and looked at me through those tight-shut eyes and I felt a deep peace take the place of fear. God was with us. Hermanito placed the bone inside the hole, then turned the knife upside down and with the blunt side hammered the bone into place. There was a dull squishing sound as it thudded against the wet raw flesh. Mr. Smith groaned. He was in pain.

"Keep him talking, little one!" Hermanito ordered the woman by Mr. Smith's side. "He must not pass out!" Hermanito's voice was urgent. He cut out a second piece of bone inside the back and repeated the process.

"Are you watching closely, little daughter?" Hermanito asked me softly. I nodded affirmatively.

"This poor man," Hermanito said. "No wonder he has been in pain. There is a small tumor at the bone of his spine."

Again the knife went into the wound. Suddenly an incredible stench filled the room. Instinctively I lifted my hand up to my face, but Hermanito grabbed it and placed it back inside the wound. "Hold the tissue taut, little daughter. I must remove this tumor. It is cancerous." He cut something loose just above my fingers and pulled out a round, stringy mass of flesh about the size of a golfball which he then wrapped in cotton to be disposed of. Hermanito took a large piece of cotton which I handed him and swept the bloody cotton aside, passing his hand over the wound. It closed as he did so.

We wrapped Mr. Smith with a piece of sheet, as in the confusion of the night no one had thought to bring a regular bandage. Hermanito supervised for a few minutes and then announced he was leaving. We lifted Mr. Smith onto the bed. The pain he had been feeling before the operation was gone and there was new fresh color in his face. He was smiling and talking. Yes, he had felt Hermanito working inside his back; he had felt pain, but he was fine now.

Several of us went into the living room for coffee. Pachita was watching me intently. Suddenly the look in her eyes changed. It was as though flames were leaping out at me. For a moment I flashed back at the eyes I had seen at Playmakers. She leaned forward and spoke to me in an unknown tongue. It sounded like Nahuatl. Then as suddenly as the spirit had appeared, it was gone. Pachita took my hand and asked where my mother was. Mama had come into the City with me that day to—reluctantly—witness the operation with me. I introduced her to Pachita.

"You are a fortunate mother. Your daughter has a very special mission in life. She will one day be able to heal even as I do. You must begin preparing yourself to help her in case an emergency should arise. She will have great need of you." Mama was almost as stunned as I was. I had not mentioned to her or anyone else besides Padre Humberto what Hermanito had told me. Now a public announcement had been made of it.

Later that night I went back with Pachita to her home. Once there, she gave me a bottle of red herbal liquid and told me to be sure Mr. Smith drank some of it for two days. He was to keep the bandage on for three days, rest in bed, and eat no pork whatever during this time.

When we returned to the house, I gave Mr. Smith a glass of the liquid. He was happy and excited. He got up and walked slowly to the bathroom and back. I saw that his new yellow pajamas were stained with blood in the back, as was his bandage and the bed sheets. His wife and I changed the sheets and his pajamas and put him back to bed. It was past 3:30 in the morning.

❀

I lay in bed thinking about the things I had seen. Was it possible it had all been a trick? Had it all been sleight of hand and a fraud? Had I been hypnotized? The replacement of the vertebrae was medically impossible. But my face was only inches from the wound. I myself had placed the strips of cotton I had cut on his skin. No one else had handled them. And I had a clear view of Pachita's hands, which were open, fingers spread. Nothing was palmed in them. At no time did she pull anything out from under her tunic; the dress she wore had no pockets anyhow. And I had felt the warm blood pulse over my hands. My hands were *in* the wound—blood was smeared to my wrists from it. But what she did was impossible!

That's right—for any human doctor. But the being working through Pachita was not human. He was supernatural—he was beyond the realm of physical laws as we know them, as so the effect and works which he performed were also supernatural and not bound by conventional rules. The spiritists are right then, I thought to myself. We are surrounded by the souls of those who have gone on. Some have reached a higher plane than others, some, perhaps even Hermanito, are closer to God, and can therefore produce wonderful miracles. Others were unquestionably evil and cruel like the horrors with which I had been acquainted for so long. Many of those whom these evil ones succeed in possessing have become incurably insane and are locked forever in asylums. "That probably would have been my fate if not for Mind Control and Hermanito," I added to myself. But those holy ones who choose to interlock their disembodied spirits with a human body which acted as a medium for them could indeed perform wonders and miracles. Kim was wrong. This work of Pachita's was not satanic. How could it be? For years I had experienced the workings of those tied to Satan. Now I was experiencing the workings of God. The *feeling* between the two was so totally different. I could tell the difference. Was there not a crucifix on the altar and a picture of Jesus? I had seen nuns and priests there, sprinkling holy water throughout the room and reciting the rosary. All glory was given to "My Father and Lord"; we were constantly told to elevate our thoughts to God and to say the Lord's Prayer. Besides, what purpose would Satan have in healing and doing good works and in casting out "devils"—as Dr. Carlos had told me happened, and which I was soon to witness. Dr. Carlos was no credulous fool, either. He was a respected surgeon with his own practice and a large pharmaceutical company. He had for several months now been working as one of Pachita's principal assistants, as I had done that night. He had assisted in dozens of operations and was in constant amazement at what he had seen Hermanito do. No, there was no question in my mind that what Pachita did was supernatural and found its ulimate source in God. I was therefore determined I should work there to learn and serve as best I could. I praised God again and again for having led me there.

❀

Mom and I drove back to Cuernavaca the next morning. That night the Padre and I met for our last session. My sense of excitement and anticipation was high. I had seen awesome things and my mission had been confirmed. It was during this meeting that I would become a full-trance medium as Hermanito had predicted.

The now familiar procedures were followed. I went to level and waited. Suddenly I felt myself sinking deeper and deeper. I felt something deep within me wrench away; my body seemed to fade. I looked down and could see my empty shell sitting straight in a chair—hands floating palms up. I was aware of being far away in a new space beyond where I had been before. I had passed through a deep darkness, but now everything was filled with a pure white light. I now fully understood that my essence, my spirit did *not* have to be tied down into the sack of flesh beneath me. It had been given me for a while to facilitate the work which lay ahead, to help fulfill my karma and purify my spirit so it could rejoin God. But I, I was eternal, an inseparable part of the Living Force.

Thoughts like these had come to me before. But now, floating far above, I was *experiencing* it. I was filled with ecstasy; there was no time, no sorrow, no pain, only vibrating unbearable joy and light and peace beyond anything I had yet experienced. I looked down. A silent, incandescent figure stood by my body waiting . . .waiting . . .yet not possessing me. Then from a great distance I heard an earthly voice calling to me. I couldn't understand the words at first, but they persisted.

"Johanna, Johanna—come back—it's time to come back—it's time to rest." Oh, it was so hard to obey that voice. It was so beautiful where I was, and I wanted to go on. But I was drawn back. I felt my body again; it was like lead and drained of all energy. Padre Humberto touched my hands gently and they dropped like dead weight in my lap. I lay back in the chair, unable to move.

"Why did you call me back so soon? We've only just started. I wasn't ready to come back." But we had been working for over an hour.

After this I frequently experienced similar things during my meditations—a sudden detachment from my body, a sense of floating far off, and I could see spirits hovering around my body, many of them evil who wanted to harm it; but other beings, benevolent and beautiful. I called them my guardian angels and knew they were protecting me from the evil ones. I felt safe and unafraid.

My sensitivity and psychic awareness had increased greatly. Yet I knew for a fact I was not a full-trance medium. I was deeply disappointed. Perhaps I just had not developed far enough. Although Pachita treated me with great affection, I sensed a radical though subtle change in Hermanito's attitude towards me which hurt me deeply. What was it in me that was barring my progress? I was not to know the answer to that question until more than a year later, but Hermanito gave me a clue during one of the curse operations in which I was assisting. I was praying intensely as Hermanito cut open a women's abdomen when suddenly he looked up and pointed to me.

"Hurry, get her out of here. She is under attack from an evil one," he said to one of the women in the group. "Brush her down with the carnations you'll find on the altar. Hurry!"

Then he added: "It is just a precaution; she has a most powerful spirit protecting her." He looked up at me as he said this, and for a moment I was paralyzed by the hatred I saw in his face. The look was gone in a flash and I never saw it again, but the impact remained with me.

11
Signs And Wonders

To say that Papa was concerned about the turn of events in my life would be an understatement. He was pleased at the positive changes he sensed in my attitude. The depression I had been in for almost a year was gone. I had a new sense of worth and purpose. For the first time in my life I felt needed. I belonged. But Daddy couldn't know the depth of those feelings. All he could see was his much-loved daughter committing herself full-steam to working with a very strange old woman whose activities were not only weird, by all reports, but unsanctioned by the government.

"What if she's raided while you're there? You could wind up in jail! What if someone dies on her? What if you catch some horrible disease from handling those people? What if something happens to you on the road or in that awful neighborhood? You're not getting home till after one in the morning!"

I loved him for his concern, but knew I was protected. Nothing would happen to me. I could sense a special force field all around me. I learned to emanate a cocoon of energy which kept all intruders out. Many times in the subway or on the bus I would see someone leer at me and begin to approach. Invariably he would stop about three feet from me as though he had hit an invisible wall and back away, looking confused. My assurances did little to convince Daddy, and he decided to drive me in to Pachita's whenever he could. After his initial fiasco with Hermanito, however, he refused to come inside, preferring to go see a movie until I was through. It was not until Hermanito and Dr. Carlos prescribed some strange medicines for me that Daddy decided to go check things out again before allowing me to swallow any of the murky brew given me.

Daddy and Dr. Carlos liked each other on sight, which was fortunate as Daddy proceeded to corner the doctor and hit him with all the questions and doubts he had concerning Pachita and Hermanito.

"I am a doctor, Don Alberto, and a surgeon. I have my own practice. Do you think I would risk everything for something I knew was a fraud or somehow dangerous? Do you think I would stay here and risk a charge of manslaughter or, worse, murder? Not once in all the years Pachita has been doing these things has anyone ever died on her table or as a result of complications from her operations, nor has anyone assisting her caught any disease. It is true, not all on whom she operates recover their health—some die despite Hermanito's efforts. But God is sovereign and Hermanito can only do what God allows."

Dr. Carlos put his hand on Papa's shoulder.

"I have been here many months now, Don Alberto. Hermanito has honored me greatly and I am one of his main assistants at the operations. I have seen wonderful things here. Miracles! He performs wonders far beyond what medical science can accomplish.

"My colleagues would say I was lying or out of my mind if I told them what I have seen. They would protest saying what Hermanito does is physically impossible! They are right. But God is much greater, Don

Alberto, much greater. I have seen with my own eyes the operations Hermanito performs. They are from God. But stay tonight, Don Alberto. You will see for yourself."

There were six operations scheduled for that night. Four were minor ones in which a special liquid was injected into the base of the spine, Hermanito's preliminary treatment for most paralytics. The procedure took only five or six minutes.

The next operation was on a young man in his mid-twenties named Heraldo*. His mother, Marina*, a lovely, very elegant lady from a wealthy family, was assisting along with the doctor. It was she who had brought Dr. Carlos to Pachita's after her own husband had been successfully treated there.

Heraldo had been in an accident several years before in which his nose had been badly broken. Surgeons had reconstructed it, but a piece of crushed bone was lodged at the base of his nose, pressing into his skull. Because of the location the surgeons had been reluctant to remove it despite the fact that it constantly impaired his breathing and occasionally caused severe headaches.

Daddy and I moved to the foot of the cot to watch. Heraldo stretched out a sheet as his mother wiped off Hermanito's scissors with a cotton soaked in balsam and handed them to him.

"Elevate your thoughts to God, dearest brothers," Hermanito said as he raised the scissors towards the altar. Then he turned to Heraldo and pushed the point of the scissors into his forehead to the right just above the nose. He made an opening in the skin. The sound of flesh being snipped was clearly audible. Then he took his knife and firmly shoved it into the wound, pounding it through the skull with the heel of his hand. We could hear the bone crushing under the blows.

Heraldo groaned. "Do you feel pain, my son?" Hermanito asked.

"Yes, a little, Hermanito." Marina reached out to touch her son's head.

"Don't you worry. We're almost through." Hermanito reached for a piece of cotton, leaving the knife clearly sticking in Heraldo's forehead as he did so. He soaked up some blood that had accumulated in the wound around the knife. He then resumed scraping inside the head for several minutes, complaining about the difficult location of the fragments which he kept digging out and removing.

Periodically, Hermanito would discuss with Dr. Carlos, who stood at his left as the main assistant, what he was doing. "Do you see here, beloved son, how these fragments have lodged themselves?"

The doctor responded affirmatively. "This is wonderful, Hermanito," he said quietly as he bent over the boy. "It would have taken me almost an hour just to go through the bone. You have done it in minutes. That is a very delicate area close to the optic nerves. He could lose his sight if they were damaged. Truly, God is good."

After twenty minutes or so the operation was over.

"There, my son, how do you feel now?" Hermanito asked gently.

"Fine, Hermanito. I can breathe perfectly out of the right side now, but the left is still the same," he answered.

"Yes, I know, my son. In ten days, when you are stronger, we will operate on your left side."

We saw Heraldo a week later when he was in for a checkup. He told us the symptoms on the right side of his nose were gone. There was no question in his mind that Hermanito had cut through his head. He had felt pain and intense pressure inside his head during the operation and could hear and feel the bone crunching and being scraped. Several days after his operation, he had gone to his doctor, who stared in disbelief at the new X-rays. The obstruction on the right side of Heraldo's nose had indeed vanished.

After Heraldo was bandaged and carried out to the other side of the house to rest for an hour, Dr. Carlos spread a clean sheet on the cot and proceeded to remove his shirt.

"What, Carlos!" my father exclaimed. "Are you going to have an operation?"

"Yes, certainly," said the doctor. "I have developed a hernia that needs to be closed. Hermanito is going to take care of it for me now." Hermanito smiled and patted the doctor's arm. "Come, Don Alberto. You stand here beside me and watch." Daddy walked around Hermanito and stood by the doctor as he stretched out on the cot.

As always, Hermanito rubbed the area to be operated with a cotton soaked in alcohol. The knife and scissors had been cleaned with the balsam and were ready for use.

As Hermanito made the cut into the abdomen, the doctor, whose head was raised on a pillow so he could observe the procedure, began describing in medical terms what was taking place. He could see and feel everything Hermanito was doing. Once the hernia had been reached, Hermanito asked Marina for a needle and thread. She was not prepared for the request and it was several minutes before a needle and spool could be located. I watched Hermanito, eyes shut, thread the needle in one try, and then proceed to stitch up the doctor's hernia, a process the doctor compared with his own technique in similar operations.

Daddy was awed. He had gone fully expecting and looking to detect fraud on one level or another and instead had witnessed at point blank two amazing operations, each verified by a practicing surgeon.

Dr. Carlos wasn't the only surgeon convinced of the reality of the phenomena that took place at Pachita's. Early in March of 1972 Dr. E. Stanton Maxey, M.D., F.A.C.S., was at Pachita's, hoping to obtain a healing for one of his terminally diseased patients. Dr. Maxey later wrote an article entitled "A Surgeon's Observation on Psychic Surgery", in which he discusses his encounter with Pachita as well as with several psychic surgeons of the Philippines. The following account is based on excerpts taken directly from that article:

In November 1971, I operated upon G.W. and removed eighteen pounds of tumor which was solid cancer (adenocarcinoma of the ovaries). There was spread of the tumor to adjacent organs which could not be removed. Conventional chemotherapy was undertaken but the remaining cancer grew. Obviously, if the patient were to survive, a miracle cure was needed.

In March I accompanied G.W., her husband, and a veterinary surgeon when a visit was made to Pachita on the outskirts of Mexico City. After several days we did manage to see her for "diagnosis." This diagnosis was something else. Each of us, upon prior instruction, presented at Pachita's home a fresh egg to be used diagnostically.

One by one, patients filed rapidly into the treatment room for their diagnoses. When our turn arrived . . . Pachita took G.W.'s egg and rapidly rolled it over the patient's head, back, and abdomen before announcing (via interpreter) that is was cancer of the uterus and then throwing the egg abruptly into an adjacent bucket. (Note: At prior surgery there was cancer invading the uterus which had not been removed.) Some of the eggs previously thrown lay burst upon the concrete floor. Pachita then put her hands into a bowl of water, sprinkled G.W. with some of it and blessed her.

...Surgery was scheduled for the following evening. This time there were fewer patients and Pachita had several assistants, one of whom accepted contributions. G.W. was put to bed in the family bedroom fully clothed and given tea to drink. Later three strong young men came and carried her prone to the treatment room together with a roll of cotton and a bottle of ethyl alcohol which we'd previously obtained. I accompanied the party.

Pachita sat before the sanctuary artifacts in very dim candlelight as G.W. was laid on the bed and her abdomen made bare. I stood at her feet, in fact I held her feet and monitored the pedal arterial pulses. Pachita splashed alcohol on the abdomen, rapidly massaged the flesh and appeared to insert both a knife and scissors deep into the abdomen with great rapidity and reckless disregard of anatomical structures. G.W. felt no pain. One heard scissors cutting away. Then it was all over and the assistants rapidly applied a bandage. Pachita sat in apparent prayer and one seemed to sense a bluish haze enveloping her and her assistants. Locally collected herbs were given to G.W. to be made into a tea for consumption upon her return home.

I changed G.W.'s dressing three days later in my office and saw only a few superficial scratches on the abdomen but I could feel warmth radiating from the entire lower abdomen as if the area alone were feverish. Her bloody dressing was examined by the Florida Department of Law Enforcement and the blood was human, type B, the patient's blood type. Dr. Maxey prefaced his account by saying:

Seeing is not believing. Seeing together with photographic documentation of the scene is still not believing. And the addition of confirmatory laboratory analysis only confuses further by posing impossibilities which are scarcely ponderable to the scientific mind.

Dr. Maxey unquestionably has a brilliant scientific mind. Besides being a practicing general surgeon for over twenty-five years and qualified by the American Board of Surgery and by fellowship in the American College of Surgeons, he is also a pilot and instrument instructor as well as an inventor who has built hydraulic operating tables, tissue processing machines, and altimeters. He also holds patents on electronic navigating and landing devices for aircraft. He states that scientific and medical experience "should be jealously guarded, for it is a very great treasure, but," he adds, "these disciplines are...not worth a fig when one ponders the imponderables of psychic surgery. ...Let me caution the reader not to expect clarifications of enigmatic mysteries. If asked I would advise that conclusions be withheld until an expanded comprehension of the phenomenal world allows a more orderly interpretation. And, since the impossibilities...described are manifestedly so, I feel safe in predicting—that a sufficient comprehension will not be seen in my lifetime."

Dr. Maxey concluded his article by saying:

I believe that academic medicine and science will disbelieve the events I've described...The pertinent question, however, is "Are patients healed?" Phenomenology aside, is there hope to be found for patients which academic medicine declares hopeless?

I know not.

But I do feel the Psychic Surgeons may help those

of us in academic medicine in our striving to perceive the 'whole cow'.

On the 15th of March 1972 I received a letter from Dr. Maxey stating that "G.W., our patient, is currently doing beautifully." On the 10th of September 1973, however, another letter from him said, "G.W. is doing poorly, though she was temporarily improved. She's now in New York receiving high energy magnetic (5,000 gans) therapy." She died in the summer of 1974.

Why wasn't G.W. healed? Stanley Krippner and Alberto Villodo, who discuss and analyze Pachita's work in their book *The Realms of Healing,* state on page 262 that the patient's world-view may have something to do with it. The discrepancy between the reality of the healer and the patient may be "one reason why tourists who show an initial improvement following psychic intervention by Doña Pachita or the Filipino spiritualists sometimes regress when they return to their homes; their temporary acceptance of the healer's belief system falls apart under scrutiny by their relatives and neighbors—and so do the benefits they attained."

That, in essence, was the explanation I myself formulated as I saw numerous patients undergo treatment and operations with little, if any, permanent healing; the person who did not experience healing was lacking in faith. When I asked Hermanito about it he confirmed that, but said that also sometimes it simply wasn't God's will for that person. Hermanito would often promise a cure or great improvement in a person's condition knowing it would not be granted but seeking nonetheless to give the person hope. "These medical doctors!" he once exclaimed in disgust. "They think they know it all! They think they are God! Who are they to say a person's case is hopeless! Perhaps it may be God's will to grant a special miracle if the person keeps hope." Then Hermanito's voice lowered and he looked away from me. "It is horrible to die and, worse, to live without hope."

❀

David* was another terminally diseased patient who was given a burst of hope by Hermanito. David and I had known each other as children. Our families had been close, especially during the years Mom and Dad had lived in Mexico City. They still kept in touch from time to time but I had not seen David for many years.

David had developed cancer sometime during his sophomore year in college. For almost two years he had undergone chemotherapy and cobalt treatments in a desperate effort to stem the disease, but now huge tumors were growing all through his body. The doctors gave him only a few months to live.

When through a mutual friend Mother heard of David's latest prognosis, she immediately called his mother to tell her of Pachita. At first Cora* was reluctant to take her son to see the old woman of whom Mama spoke so highly, but they had exhausted every other possibility. There was nowhere else to go.

I went into the room with David and stood by him as Hermanito briskly rubbed the egg over his body and felt several of the tumors. One was on the side of his neck and was almost the size of my fist. Hermanito blessed David with the balsam and then placed both hands on his shoulders. "My son, the doctors have told you you have cancer. The doctors have misdiagnosed. What you have is accumulations of fat which have grown to disproportionate size in your body. It is nothing that will kill you, little one. Take courage!

David looked up in disbelief as Hermanito prescribed a treatment for him consisting of herbal teas and *mamporro*, (a kind of snake which Pachita dried, ground up, then packaged in large gelatin capsules.) Hermanito had said nothing about an operation, which I thought unusual, but I was certain David would have one eventually and would be cured. We were both elated! We rushed outside where Mom and Cora were waiting and gave them the wonderful news.

But the treatment didn't seem to help. In fact, David's condition began to deteriorate. His pain was becoming so unbearable that even morphine shots no longer seemed to ease it. His spirits, which had been so lifted and encouraged by Hermanito's words, now fell. He began speaking desperately of suicide to put an end to the agony.

I was at Pachita's on the morning of the 29th of February 1971 when David's father, Andrew* arrived. "Johanna, I'm so glad you are here!" he exclaimed, taking my hands. "I have David in the car. He is not well, Johanna. His pain is unbearable. He says if Hermanito doesn't operate on him now he will kill himself." There were tears in his eyes as he spoke.

"Wait here, Andrew. I'll get Pachita."

Pachita leaned into the car to talk to David, who lay doubled up in the back seat. Her face was troubled as she and I stepped inside the courtyard to talk. "Pachita, will Hermanito operate on him now? You see how he is."

"Ay, Johanna, I don't know," Pachita answered. "The boy's cancer is too far advanced. I do not think he would survive an operation now."

"Cancer! But Pachita, Hermanito said it was not cancer!"

Pachita shook her head. "It is cancer. Hermanito knew no treatment would work for the boy at all if he had no hope. Who knows but God would grant a miracle. But he's too far gone now. What if he should die while he's here!"

"Pachita, Hermanito *must* operate. David can no longer stand the pain. Please, will you ask him?"

"Very well, we will ask him," she said, shaking her head doubtfully. "Come."

We went into the altar room. Hermanito arrived minutes later.

"We will operate on the boy," he said slowly after several moments of silence. "It will be in God's hands to save him if it is His will." Hermanito turned to me.

"For three days you must do the following for him in preparation." Hermanito's voice became brisk. "Find rotten mud by a stagnant stream. Heat it, then rub it over the tumor under his ribs. Bandage it and leave it on as long as he can stand it; several hours at least and preferably overnight. This will help concentrate the virus so it can be removed. In the morning rub his chest and back and tumors on his neck with this sweet smelling balsam mixed with chinese cabbage." (He gave me the name of a certain ointment.) He paused for a moment and then took my hand, "It may be, little one, that you will be instrumental in his healing. Again I tell you, you have a gift. You will heal someday even as my flesh does. Take this bottle of balsam. At night when the family is asleep, go into each room of the house and sprinkle it around you as you invoke the name of God. If his parents' door is closed, sprinkle water on it. Then take a glass of pure water. Go out to the balcony, raise it high in your right hand and say 'May the most precious blood of our Lord Jesus Christ which when only represented in Egypt brought freedom to the Israelites by the strong arm of God, free us and favor us against all evil. Amen.' Then recite the Lord's Prayer. Put the glass on the floor. You will keep it there all night. Then lift both hands high above you in supplication and say, 'Father, my Lord, in this instant I ask you to bless these hands which you have given me.

They are empty now, Lord, but by your great love, enable and fill them with charity to remove from this body every trace of illness. By your divine goodness, I give you thanks, Great Lord.'

"'Light and Light; Sun and Earth, Moon and Stars, Plants and Mosses, Reptiles of the Earth; Seas and Rivers; Women and Tribes from all the confines of the Earth in conjunction and harmony I ask of you this day the health of this patient.'

"Then again repeat the Lord's Prayer. David is to drink the water you left out in the elements first thing in the morning. Have you understood all I have said to you, little one?"

"Yes, Hermanito, I have."

"Then go with God. And plead with Him for the boy's life."

We took David home and put him to bed while his father and I drove to the outskirts of the city where we found a large stagnant pool of water that had once been part of the Aztec canal system. We filled a large bucket with the stinking mud.

I had David stretch out on a towel as I heated the mud. Little white maggots collected on the surface of the slime. I lifted out all the ones I could find with a spoon and then applied the mud to David's abdomen. He submitted quietly to the horror, knowing that Hermanito had promised an operation.

Only five operations were scheduled for the night of March 2nd. David's was to be the last. Mama and Daddy, David's father, and a friend of the family gathered in the room. Chalio and I were assisting. We spread the sheet David's father had brought and had him stretch out upon it. Chalio helped him unbutton his shirt. Hermanito looked down at him.

"Don't worry, my son, everything will be as God ordains." I handed Hermanito a block of cotton soaked in alcohol which he rubbed briskly over David's abdomen. Then he placed four cotton pieces around the area to be operated on the right side of the chest below the ribs. He took the scissors I handed him.

"Form a circle around him, dearest brothers. Hold hands and pray; pray with all your strength that God grant us this boy's healing." He raised the scissors in prayer for a long moment, then plunged them into David's side. He cut for a few moments, then asked "Do you feel pain, little one?" David didn't answer. The tension suddenly increased in the room. Hermanito pulled the scissors out and looked at David's face. He looked as though he were dead. I could no longer feel his chest rising or falling. Hermanito's breath drew in sharply as he grabbed Chalio's arm.

"Roll up your sleeve. We must perform a transfusion. Hurry! The rest of you pray!" he ordered. Hermanito grabbed Chalio's bare arm and ran his index finger down the skin, which opened and began bleeding. Instantly, he did the same to David and held the two arms together for about thirty seconds. I could hear Hermanito's voice murmuring what seemed to be a prayer, but in a foreign tongue, as his tightly shut eyes stared at David's face.

Then, suddenly, David took a deep breath and opened his eyes. "There, there," said Hermanito very softly. "To my God be thanks. You have Yaqui blood in you now, my son. We may continue." He took the knife and cut out a large tumor, which he wrapped in sheets of dark paper. His hand rested on David's wound for several seconds, after which he swept away the blood-soaked cotton and covered the area with a clean pad. "We have finished, dearest brothers. Bandage him now and take him out to rest."

Chalio, Andrew, and Daddy helped carry David out of the room; everyone else followed to see after him. I was alone in the room with Hermanito, who stood by the altar. Suddenly he covered his face and began sobbing. They were tears of fear mingled with relief.

"Hermanito—Hermanito what is the matter?" I asked, my heart breaking at the depth of his sobs.

"Oh my little one, I am becoming such a coward." David had died on the table that night. The force behind Hermanito had brought him back to life, but the call had been too close.

12
Pachita

Strings of dessicated snake lay on the table in the living room. One by one Pachita picked them up, put them in a small stone bowl and, with a well-worn pestle, firmly ground them to a fine powder.

"I hope this will be enough," Pachita sighed as she surveyed the meager contents of the bowl. "It will have to do in any case. This was all the *mamporro*, the *hiervero* (herbalist), could find for me. These doggone animals are getting scarce these days. You wouldn't believe what he charged me for *this* one!"

"Isn't there anything else Hermanito could use as a substitute?" I asked as I carefully filled the large gelatin capsules with the powder.

"Not for certain kinds of cancer," she answered, shaking her head. "*Mamporro* capsules are the most effective...but only if started early enough. Most people who come to Hermanito are too far gone." She sighed again as she placed another snake strip into her bowl. I wondered if she was thinking of David as she said it. It had been several weeks since his operation. He seemed to be much better, but it was still too soon to tell.

We worked in silence for a few minutes.

"Pachita...would you mind if I asked you something personal?" I said, hesitantly.

"Of course not, little daughter," she smiled, glancing up at me.

"How did you begin with Hermanito?"

Pachita said nothing for several seconds as she continued grinding. "I was abandoned by my parents when I was a baby," she said quietly. "A little black man from the Yucatan Peninsula adopted me. He took care of the animals in a circus. I trained as a trapeze artist, but what I really loved was working with the animals. I had a special gift with them—knew what they felt, knew instinctly how to cure them when they were sick.

"For example, one night one of the elephants was having a terrible time giving birth to her calf. No one knew what to do. It looked as though both the elephant and her baby would die. I was standing there watching when something came over me. I knew how to help the animal. I gave exact instructions for what had to be done. Both mother and calf were saved. The vet was very confused," she laughed. "Here was a nine year old little girl telling *him* what to do!"

Pachita paused and rubbed her neck for a moment. "Here, you grind for a while, I'm tired."

I pulled the stone bowl over to my side of the table and reached for another piece of snake. Pachita took a deep breath as she rubbed her face, then continued.

"I didn't begin working as a full-trance medium until my late twenties. One day, at three o'clock in the afternoon, I became tired...so tired...and I fell asleep. For months this happened; at three o'clock I would fall asleep wherever I was. When I'd wake up I would have the sense that spirits had come to me to teach me about herbs and ancient treatments and things. Then one afternoon a spirit took possession of me. He announced that he had come to be my guide and that we were to call him "Hermanito." He said that in life he had been known as *Cuauhtemoc*. His mission on earth as a healer and leader had been cut short when the Spaniards killed him. He and I would heal together, he said, for this was my mission in this life.

"He began to diagnose the illnesses of whoever happened to be there, and to prescribe herbs and cures for them.

"One evening I awoke from my trance to find my hands covered in fresh blood. You can't imagine the fright that gave me! I was told that Hermanito had looked at a patient, announced he needed an operation and had cut him open with a kitchen knife. The patient felt no pain and recovered from his illness, but the people were frightened. They said I was insane and locked me in an asylum for two years."

Her face reflected the horror of those years and her voice was bitter.

"Finally they let me out. I married and had five children. Two of them are dead now. They got sick and died."

"But Pachita, couldn't Hermanito help them?" I exclaimed, surprised.

"Oh, yes," she answered softly, "but he wouldn't. He said that it was God's will they leave this earth, that it was for the sake of karma that I needed to suffer their loss. I was so furious with Hermanito, I wouldn't allow him to come to me for weeks, but he finally wore me down with his persistence.

"Then my husband left me. He couldn't take it anymore—our children's death, all the people here at all hours of the day and night, no privacy or life of our own. You've seen what it's like here, little daughter." I nodded. She seldom, if ever, had a moment to herself. There was always someone at her door seeking Hermanito's help. I never saw her turn anyone away.

"So, little daughter, there you have it. Hermanito has been with me for forty-six years now. He has performed marvelous healings through me, but I don't know for how much longer. I am old and I am sick and I am very tired, Johanna. My energy level is not what it used to be. It makes it harder for Hermanito to operate successfully. I don't imagine I have many more years of usefulness left in me...that is why you must not become discouraged and must continue to study and work. My sons have refused my mantle. They are too busy with their own things to sacrifice themselves in this work. It will fall to you, little one, for you are gifted and willing. I will teach you all I know."

"Then Pachita, why is it that..." my question was cut off by the arrival of a young woman holding a desperately sick child in her arms. Never again did the time seem right to ask Pachita why, if I had been chosen, I was not yet working as a full-trance medium as Hermanito had said I would. I put the pestle down and followed Pachita into the altar room.

✹

The child shrieked in pain and terror as Hermanito cut a deep slit in the back of his tiny neck.

"We're almost through, my little one," Hermanito said soothingly to the boy. "Try to keep him still just a moment longer," he said to the child's mother. "It won't be much longer. Hand me that jar there by you, my daughter...yes, that's the one." I took the lid off a small jar and held it as he fished out a two-inch-long tube.

"Hold the boy's head still, Chalio!" he ordered as he placed the tube inside the boy's neck at the base of the skull. The boy wailed as Hermanito's fingers went into his flesh. Then he carefully placed a clean block of cotton on the wound.

"We have finished, dearest brothers. The tube will help drain the excess fluid from his brain. The boy will recover." The child's mother fell on her knees before Hermanito and reached for his hand to kiss it.

"God bless you, Hermanito, you are a saint. Thank you—thank you!" Tears of gratitude streamed down her cheeks.

"Rise, little one. Do not thank me. All thanks belong to my father above." The mother hurried to the child's side as he was wrapped in a sheet and carried out.

"Chalio, dearest one, come here. I have a surprise for you." Hermanito sat on the chair near the altar. The operations were over for that night.

"Tell me, my son," he said solemnly as he stretched out Pachita's hands before him and studied them critically, "how many times have I told you people not to permit my flesh to wear this ghastly nail polish?"

Everyone in the room laughed. "Oh, many, many times, Hermanito," Chalio chuckled.

"But she insists on ignoring me, does she not, and not *one* of you is brave enough to say anything about it to her! Give me your hands!" he ordered, looking stern. He had reached behind him and taken a small bottle of deep purple nail polish off the table. Chalio started to hide his hands behind his back, suspecting what Hermanito was up to, but Hermanito grabbed one and deftly began painting Chalio's nails.

"Aha!" he laughed merrily. "A work of art, is it not! Now you have some idea, dearest brothers, how I feel when I arrive to find my hands in such a degrading state. That goes for these frivolous female hair combs too," he exclaimed, pulling them from his hair and waving them before us. "May this be a lesson to you all!"

❁

"No, the cot is not stable enough for this operation,"

Hermanito announced the next night as I smoothed Perry's sheet upon it.

"We will need the table from the living room for this one." Dr. Carlos and Chalio brought the table in and stood it in the center of the room. I covered it with the sheet, helped Perry* stretch out on it, then transferred the bowls and stacks of cotton, along with two styrofoam boxes filled with miscellaneous supplies which ranged from suction tubes to talcum powder, to the edge of the cot behind me. The knife and scissors had been wiped clean after the last operation and lay ready beside the cotton.

Perry was a former army officer who had lived in Mexico since his retirement. For several years now he had suffered from an inoperable brain tumor which had increasingly tormented him with blinding headaches and nausea. The pain had become almost unbearable over the years and he was sure he didn't have long to live.

"Tell him to lie on his side facing you, my daughter," Hermanito instructed me. "Hold his hand and keep him talking." Hermanito stood behind Perry, with Dr. Carlos beside him. Hermanito extended his hand and I placed a small block of alcohol-saturated cotton in it. He rubbed it all over the top of Perry's head. Again he extended a hand and I reached for the scissors.

"No, little one, hand me the knife first time." In a single, violent motion he plunged it into Perry's skull.

The man on the table gasped.

"Do you feel pain, Perry?" I asked him anxiously.

"Oh, no," he replied with a faint smile, "but I can feel something moving inside my head—it's so strange!" he laughed nervously.

Hermanito worked inside the head for several minutes, snipping and cutting with the scissors I handed him. Then, a stench, like the kind I had smelled so often during cancer operations, rose from the gaping hole in Perry's head as Hermanito pulled a stringy, dripping blob and dropped it into a large piece of cotton Dr. Carlos held for him.

"I can't see very well," Perry said just as the wound was about to be closed. Hermanito looked up at me.

"Little one, look into Perry's eyes...have they become crossed?" They had. Totally.

"Well, that certainly won't do, will it!" Hermanito reached a hand back into the skull—and Perry's eyes snapped back to their normal position.

Several days after the operation, I called him to see how he was doing. He told me his headaches were completely gone for the first time in years, as was his nausea. He was eating and gaining weight. His color was back. In short, he felt wonderful. In fact, even the toothache he had during the operation had been healed that night. Almost a year later when Daddy ran into him, he reported he was still doing beautifully. None of the old symptoms had returned.

Don Ignacio, a notary public, is another person who experienced complete healing at Hermanito's hands. For three years he had been plagued by painful indigestion caused by a benign tumor located at the lower end of his stomach where it empties into the intestines. It had grown so large I could see a lump in his side when he removed his shirt before lying on the cot. Daddy helped arrange the pillow under the old gentleman's head.

"Don't worry about me, Don Alberto," he said to his old friend with a confident, peaceful smile. "I will be just fine. Hermanito has a direct line to the Divine Source. Nothing can go wrong."

"This brother understands," Hermanito observed with an approving smile. "It is good."

Don Ignacio's operation was an unqualified success.

The lump in his side, along with all the symptoms, vanished, never to return.

Bob's experience, however, was not so fortunate. He had been wounded in action during the Korean war and left a paraplegic. Although skeptical, he decided to visit Pachita as word of her powers spread through the American community.

Hermanito's verdict on Bob's condition stunned us; the situation was not hopeless. It would take patience on his part, and at least two operations to replace the dead nerves in his spine, but he would walk.

His first operation took place on the night before David was told he did not have cancer.

Bob's operation was a painful one. I never could understand why some who sat under Hermanito's knife felt no pain, while others suffered almost unbearable agony. But he bore it and for the next weeks faithfully followed the prescribed routine of therapy and post-operative teas which Hermanito stressed were vital to nourish the newly implanted nerve. From time to time he would enthusiastically report a new sensation in his legs and feet, and I, convinced he would soon be walking, encouraged him to have faith and persevere.

Bob's second operation was, if anything, more painful than the first. I was certain this was a good sign—an indication of restored feeling in his back. For the second time we drove him home to Cuernavaca face down on a mattress in our station wagon, but this time without the precious tea. The hiervero had been late in the delivery of a vital ingredient. It would be ready on the next day. But somehow signals were crossed, and Bob never received it. All progress came to a halt, and Bob remained in his chair.

Similarly, author and poetess Virginia Hammond* had ruptured two disks in her back after slipping on a throw rug one night after a dance. She was seventeen years old at the time. She had spent years in constant, agonizing pain, and had undergone sixteen operations—four severe ones—on her spine before seeing Hermanito. She recounts:

I had read of so-called "psychic operations" performed in various parts of the world in which the healer operated on the etheric—that is, the invisible "body." I thought this would be similar, so I, like many others, went to Pachita hoping to be healed. However, when I found out just what kind of operation she planned to do on me, I had grave doubts and misgivings. I had an uneasy feeling about Hermanito during my diagnostic session with him. There was something wrong, even sinister, about the presence I felt there.

But Tom (from Mind Control) and several other friends convinced me, from their past experiences and observations, that Hermanito was a most benevolent entity. They assured me my miraculous operation would take only a few minutes, that the wound would heal immediately, and that I would experience no pain. So I decided not to let my intuition sway me. I wish to God I had. Hell could not be worse than what I experienced that night.

The night I arrived for my operation, Hermanito showed me a jar with several vertabrae from a cadaver that he said he would exchange for my damaged ones. I had paid 2,000 pesos in advance for them.

As I stretched out on my face on the cot, Hermanito again assured me I would feel no pain. But then I felt the knife go into my back—down into my spine. The pain was searing, hideous. I screamed and screamed but it wouldn't stop. At least four times I felt his fingers pull something out of my back, then suddenly push something sharp and hard into it and hammer it into place.

I kept screaming—screaming to God. I knew suddenly I was in the hands of great evil. I felt intense hatred from him towards me. The only explanation I have for that is that I am very committed to Christ; Hermanito must have sensed that.

Finally it was over and I was carried out of the altar room by several men. I had been told the wound would close instantly after the operation, but the gap in my back did not heal. It was over ten inches long and several inches deep. It became infected and bled for months. My daughter cleaned it for me as best she could; I was too afraid and ashamed to go to my doctor, knowing he scoffs at such things.

After months of intense pain, illness, and prayer, the wound finally closed, but I was never healed. On the contrary, the condition of my spine became much worse after the operation. The only miracle was that I lived through this terrible experience at all; and that, I believe, was due to God's help in answer to prayer.

13
Exodus

By September 1972 I had been working with Pachita for over fourteen months. I had washed the blood of over 200 operations from my hands. I had seen everything from the removal of brain tumors to the replacement of vertebrae and lung transplants. I had seen things materialize and removed from the human body during *daño* (curse) operations which further defied belief and logical explanation: handfuls of live worms scooped from one woman's stomach; a white arrowhead from another's heart; a black furry rock the size of a child's fist pried from the throat of a singer, who, for no apparent reason had from one day to the next lost her voice; another rock, large and covered with long black hair which appeared to be growing out of the pores removed from a man's kidneys; yards of hideously rotten, bloody, mud-covered rags which I helped Hermanito and Dr. Carlos unravel from a woman's abdomen.

Even Mom and Dad had assisted in one of these. A boy, no older than sixteen or seventeen, was brought in by his family for an operation. He had been dumb from birth. The doctors had been unable to offer any reason for his condition. Hermanito explained to the

family that a powerful curse had been placed on the
child, while still in his mother's womb, by a jealous
relative who could bear no children. Tonight the curse
which bound the boy's throat would be unlocked.

He was instructed to sit in the chair facing the altar.

"Come, Don Alberto. You will assist me along with
the dear doctor in this operation."

Daddy looked startled, but moved to Hermanito's
side. Mother hovered in the background, clutching her
purse to her chest. I knew she didn't want to be there.
From the beginning she could sense the swirling
presence of the spirits, and it frightened her. She had
also voiced objections about the singing of hymns to
Hermanito, and on several occasions when the name
of God was invoked she said she had heard him mutter
to himself "soy yo, soy yo" - ("It is I, it is I"). She had
also been there the night of David's operation; she
knew that he had died and only barely been brought
back to life. The place terrified her. But from time to
time Hermanito would insist I bring her with me and
the suspected possible consequence of refusing his
summons was more frightening to her than actually attending.

Hermanito slashed the boy's throat open, then took
Daddy's hand and pushed it into the gaping hole.

"There, do you feel that lump in there, Don
Alberto?" Daddy nodded. "Good, good—now, when
you feel it loosen, pull it out. Go on! Don't be afraid!"

Daddy pulled out a squirming bloody lump of matter, which was wrapped by the doctor in dark paper,
bound with string and placed upon the altar. Then
Hermanito's hand was back in the wound.

"I need a tiny key. Someone in this room has one!"

No one moved.

"Come now, dearest children. We can't stand here
like this all night! It's in your purse," he added to no

one in particular.

"Oh! *I* have it!" Mama exclaimed excitedly. She pulled a bunch of keys from her purse; among them was a tiny brass key.

Hermanito took the key, pushed it into the hole and turned it.

After the boy was bandaged, Hermanito commanded him to speak. "Come on now, say after me: 'Pachita.' " After a long moment the boy, hesistantly, hoarsly, spoke his first word: "Pa-chi-ta."

The boy's family burst into tears at the sound.

"Wonderful! Now the doctor's name—Dr. Carlos . . . that's it! Now say Don Roberto's name" (*"Alberto"* Daddy corrected) and even Daddy's eyes filled with tears as the boy joyfully sounded out his name. The curse had been unlocked.

❀

Twelve people were almost always called to form a half circle around the cot and pray to God for protection during the curse operations. The objects removed were always wrapped in dark paper, bound with string and covered with a leather thong studded with bells. The evil package, thus bound, was then laid upon the holy altar from where it could do no further harm.

"You see, my little one," Hermanito once explained to me, "a person who wishes another one evil strongly enough can often cause dark beings to focus upon him. They can wound his spirit with arrows or rocks or living worms and snakes—with many things which can bring great harm to the victim's body and mind. By God's power I materialize this evil within the body and remove it. At midnight my flesh takes the foul thing to the mountains where we force the dark ones to give up their curse." Hermanito sighed. "They don't know what they do. May God grant them enlightenment."

Dr. Carlos later told me of the sessions which he

sometimes attended on the mountainside; spiritual battles in which frequently those standing in the prayer circle around the fire would be pelted from out of nowhere with rocks and filth or gunpowder which would drop down upon the group. Sometimes it covered all but one or two people before the dark package was buried or cast into the fire.

"You can sometimes hear the spirits wailing furiously in the night. It is best that you not go," Dr. Carlos had told me. I agreed with him. Despite my curiosity and desire to learn, I had no real wish to encounter these entities any more than I already had.

There was yet time to learn of bringing the dark ones to light. Perhaps more to the point, I felt I wasn't yet worthy of doing so. Despite all I had learned in the last year, I was not a full-trance medium as Hermanito had said I would be. I was not growing as I should, as I knew Hermanito had expected me to. He had said nothing to me about my failure, but I could sense his disappointment and I felt vaguely ashamed and uneasy.

But there were other things that troubled me as well. David was dead. Hermanito had said that David would live, yet less than four months after his operation, he died of cancer. I was also finding that other cures Hermanito performed were only temporary. Perhaps as Pachita herself had implied, she was getting old and sick, but maybe, I thought, it was because she was compromising her stand on money and was now allowing some of those around her to charge large sums for her services and medicines.

I also couldn't understand why Hermanito, despite his humor about it, treated Pachita so cruelly—never allowing her any new or pretty clothes, and refusing to treat her when she was sick, which was often now. Even "karma" seemed a poor excuse for that. And her family was falling apart around her. Over the months, what peace I had perceived there deteriorated in the presence of almost constant tension and bickering among her children.

Things had become too hectic. The vision was no longer as clear as it had seemed when I first arrived. I needed to get away for a while, to spend time alone where I could commune with God and find my way again.

❀

I went to say goodbye the morning of September 7.

"Ah, it is good to see you, I have missed you these past weeks. Are you well?" Pachita patted my shoulders as I came in the gate. "Come. Have some coffee with me." We went into the tiny kitchen and I sat at the familiar old table. Pachita poured a mug of steaming coffee and milk from a clay jar and lowered herself onto the chair next to me. "It's good you have come, Johanna. Hermanito has left word he will operate tonight after all."

"I can't stay, Pachita."

Pachita put her mug down and looked at me.

"I'm going away for a while—to England. I've come to ask your blessing and Hermanito's."

"How long will you be gone, daughter?"

"Only two months or so, Pachita. I'll be back then."

Pachita looked at me a long moment and said nothing. I took her hands.

"Will you keep me in your prayers, Pachita?"

"I will, daughter, of course. And I will ask Hermanito to look after you," she added quietly. "I give you my blessing. Go with God."

I kissed her on the cheek and left.

The months that followed are filled with images of velvet green English meadows guarded by ancient castles and dark towers; stone grey, cold cathedrals echoing the feet of long-dead pilgrims; white marble tombs and deep jewel-colored glass; the sense of brooding evil that filled Winchester Cathedral—a glimpse of cowled monks and the smell of death; the silken sighs and rustling that filled my lonely room in the middle of the night; the shock of terror as I opened the bathroom door at my hostel in Edinburgh one night to see a paunchy man lying dead in the tub, head back, throat slashed, gashes in his chest, blood everywhere. The scene faded from my sight even as I backed away.

I hurried to my room, bolted the door behind me and dropped to my knees beside my bed. "God, I know you are with me—I know you are protecting me, but Lord Jesus, I'm so confused—why am I feeling so afraid again? Why am I again seeing horrors like this? Oh, God, protect me—guide me. I'm in Your hands, Father. Please, give me Your holy peace." My body was shaking, but no tears would come. I fell asleep clutching a tiny pewter angel I carried with me everywhere and I moved to another hostel early the next morning.

Eventually I found my way to Florence, Italy to see my sister, who had been living there for several months since her graduation from college that summer. Quite frankly I had mixed emotions about visiting her. I missed her, and yet painfully vivid memories of heated theological discussions leaped to mind. As a committed Christian, Kim was certain all my pet activities, namely Yoga, (I had been teaching Hatha Yoga and learning Raja Yoga for about a year), Mind Control, and psychic surgery, were of the devil, and said so. I was equally assured of the fact that she, on the other hand, was a narrow-minded, bigoted, Bible-thumping evangelical, who wouldn't know a genuine miracle from God if it ran her down in the street. After all, I had spent much of my life terrorized by evil beings. I *knew* what their source was. But now, through meditation, Pachita and my counselors, I was seeing wonderful things, miraculous operations, hope restored, evil spirits cast out. Granted, there were a few discrepancies I couldn't explain, but nevertheless Satan couldn't heal, could he? And surely he wouldn't cast out demons. After all, didn't the Scriptures state that a house divided against itself cannot stand? I had experienced evil; I had felt the presence of the Holy. I could tell the difference. What Pachita did had to be from God.

I had been in Florence with Kim for only a few days when, not altogether unexpectedly, the general thread of this conversation was soon picked up and we were off again. This time, however, Kim's tactics took a slightly different bent. She asked questions—questions which now began echoing some of my own hidden doubts.

"You say you can tell the difference between good and evil spirits, but how can you be sure your senses haven't been deceived?" "Yes, Pachita performs amazing operations, but how do you know for sure her source of power is God?" "You say you believe in Jesus—but which one?" "How do you know the Jesus you see in your laboratory is the Jesus of the Bible?" "How do you know demons are truly being cast out. Is it possible they are play-acting?"

I had to admit, if only to myself, I didn't really know. The only argument I could fall back on was my experience—my feelings and perceptions. Yes, I had read and studied the masters, Edgar Cayce, Allan Kardec. I could give eloquent explanations when asked about reincarnation, karma and cosmic consciousness and astral planes and psychic manifestations. But when it came right down to it, I knew there was no solid, truly objective way of testing the source behind them, and that troubled me. How *could* I be sure the source was God? I had no absolutes against which to compare my experience.

My philosophy was admittedly mongrel in texture. I had taken whatever element happened to appeal to me from Hinduism, Spiritism and Christianity and casually discarded the rest. The approach hadn't appeared inconsistent at the time. After all, there are almost as many versions of these philosophies as there are adherents (and besides, in a relativistic universe is not any path to God valid "so long as you're sincere?"). In my case, my own particular syncretism worked for me. It seemed to provide the simplest, most logical answers to so many of my questions.

The practice of yoga had given discipline and structure to my life. Hours of exercise and meditation were opening my mind and spirit to a closer realization of my unity with the Light of God—with the consciousness of the Christ force, and that realization filled me with a confidence and a peace I had never before experienced. I didn't have to be a helpless pawn in the hands of undeveloped wicked forces. I could be in control of my own destiny if I worked at it long and hard enough. I could purge my karma and break the endless cycle of incarnations. During meditation vivid scenes of at least fifteen different incarnations had filled my mind, expanding and adding to those I perceived years before giving me a deeper understanding of what I needed to sacrifice and suffer in order to achieve perfect unity with God.

My work as a medium with Pachita was a perfect vehicle for me to achieve this. Highly developed spirits, such as Hermanito Cuauhtemoc, would use and guide me in my path towards God. I felt blessed to have been chosen by them to witness such awesome power.

But above all stood my belief in Jesus Christ. He was

my guru, my guide, counselor and Lord; the Holy One of God who stood far beyond all other *avatars* (incarnations of deities); the One who deigned to come into my psychic laboratory to commune with me, giving me visions of inexpressable ecstacy. He was my ultimate way to God through His teachings and example...but not necessarily everyone's way. A man could find no greater path—no dearer Master—but each had to seek his own way and perhaps some other Lord would suit him better in this life. How could it be otherwise in a universe filled with such vast diversity?

And yet...and yet, what if Kim was right? What if my senses had been manipulated? What if the miracles and the ecstatic visions were all designed by some vast malevolent intellect to lure me into ultimate destruction. In short, what if I was wrong?

For the first time I sat still and quiet under the gentle but insistent onslaught of Kim's questions. Finally she stopped and took my hand. "Look, Johanna, why don't you go to L'Abri in Switzerland for a few days. Os Guinness is a counselor there—he knows a lot about these things. Maybe he can help make all this clearer to you."

I looked up sharply. L'Abri!—That was the last place in the world I wanted to go. I had a run-in with Edith Schaeffer that spring in Acapulco which had been anything but pleasant or enlightening for either of us and I wasn't eager for what I assumed would be more of the same.

Dr. Schaeffer, who with his wife Edith, had founded L'Abri as a place of Christian study and ministry, was lecturing at the Young President's Organization at the Acapulco Princess Hotel. Kim begged the family to go with her to listen to him. We had long heard of the Schaeffers, for Kim had spent some time with them in Switzerland during her junior year abroad. Our curiosity got the better of us, so we went.

In obvious hope that the Schaeffers could say something that would bring Mom, Dad and me "to our senses" about Mind Control and Pachita, Kim maneuvered us into having lunch with Edith one afternoon after one of Dr. Schaeffer's lectures. The topic of conversation soon shifted from the weather to theology and the occult. As I recall, despite the reasonable gentleness of her words, I came perilously close to calling her what I had already labeled my sister; a narrow-minded, spiritually underdeveloped and undiscerning legalistic fundamentalist who simply didn't understand the vastness of the manifestations of God. Edith paled slightly under the warm Acapulco sun, but tactfully said nothing more on the subject. Nonetheless, the name L'Abri now, unfairly, conjured the distressing image of dozens of fire-and-brimstoners jumping down my throat, trying to convert me before I even got in the door.

"Don't look so distressed," Kim laughed. "I'm not asking you to move in permanently; just go for a couple of days and talk to Os. It can't hurt to listen. Besides, your train goes near the place on your way back to England anyway."

I took a deep breath. "All right. I'll go. Who knows. Maybe there *is* something for me there."

❀

To my relief the jabbering hordes I had expected on my arrival at L'Abri never materialized. Well, that first night at dinner one girl did start visibly, exclaiming: "Don't you know that's of the devil!?" in response to my inadvertent revelation that I taught yoga, but I knew she was just a guest there herself and not one of the staff, so I let it slide. At least I knew enough not to bring up Pachita, so I was allowed several days of relatively peaceful anonymity before I decided to talk to Os and Sheila Bird (the counselor with whom Kim had suggested I spend time before seeing Os).

Sunday morning, after chapel, I had someone point "Birdie" out to me. She was a small woman probably in her forties. I watched Birdie's face as she spoke with a young girl. Her eyes were stern but kind. As I moved closer, Birdie glanced over at me and stopped in mid sentence. "You must be Kim's sister!" she exclaimed. I nodded.

"Kim called several days ago. Os and I have been expecting you. Why don't you come by my chalet after lunch today for a visit."

Birdie's chalet was perched at the end of a path that wound gently along the side of a mountain. Sections of the path closely bordered along the edge. It seemed a long way down to the bottom.

My steps slowed as I neared her chalet. I was feeling a growing reluctance to talk with her and was tempted to go for a walk through the village instead. My upbringing got the better of me, however, and I arrived on time.

Birdie ushered me into a tiny, cozy room and finally, after much gentle coaxing, had me talking about the beings and manifestations that filled my life. I was telling her about my college days when Birdie said, "You know, if you had truly believed in Jesus and had known how to make use of the weapons He has provided, you wouldn't have had to go through all that."

"But I don't anymore, Birdie!" I exclaimed, "For the last year since I've been with Mind Control and yoga and Pachita I've gained control. If anything frightening appears, I just go deeper in meditation or call on Jesus or Hermanito and the evil ones disappear. I *am* learning to use God's weapons!"

Birdie just nodded. "Tell me about this Mind Control and Pachita."

She was silent for several minutes after I had finished.

"Well, Johanna, I can certainly see why you believe as you do, but something about what Pachita is doing makes me uncomfortable. Let's not talk about it just now, though. First I'd like you to spend the next day or so reading the Gospel of John and the first Epistle of John. It will help lay a foundation for our next meeting."

It seemed a reasonable request.

Back at my chalet that afternoon I settled down in a corner with a new Bible and opened to the Gospel of John.

"In the beginning was the Word, and Word was with God, and the Word was God. He was in the beginning with God. All things came into being through Him, and apart from Him..."

Suddenly I was hit by a wave of exhaustion. I had been wide awake and willing to read minutes before, but now I was so tired I literally couldn't keep my eyes open. The words all seemed to fuse together. "I'll rest a while—I can read this later," I thought. I curled up and sank into a deep sleep for several hours until someone stopped by to call me for dinner. I spent all the next day in my room trying to read, but never got past a few words before an overwhelming desire to sleep pulled me under.

By Tuesday morning's meeting with Birdie I still hadn't read past the fourth verse of John.

"Actually I'm really not surprised," Birdie said cryptically when I told her. "Look—why don't you stay here today and read. There is a different spirit in this place. I don't think you'll have any trouble staying awake this time." She was right. I had read First John and the Gospels several times in the past, but the words never had the same impact on me they had now. The Jesus I was encountering on the pages of that Bible was not only alive and real, but was filled with awesome power and majesty. A mere spoken word of healing or deliverance was sufficient to bring it about. His claim to unique incarnate Deity was unmistakable, despite what I still believed about it. Verse after verse asserted that apart from Him there was no forgiveness of sin.

I was shaken and confused by the time I finished the last verse in the Gospel of John. If what I had just read was true, then everything I believed about karma and the way to unity with God was wrong. It couldn't be both ways. The claims made by Jesus were too exclusive. And if I was wrong about what I believed about Jesus, then maybe I was wrong about the rest as well.

Despite a well-rehearsed serene exterior, I was in turmoil by the time I arrived at Os Guinness's home later that afternoon. Part of me wanted desperately to know the truth, another part of me still wanted to shut down and ignore the whole business. Os spoke to me about the irreconcilable dichotomy between the Eastern and biblical view of God, salvation, and Jesus. He said something about the physical and spiritual dangers of the occult and told me of how he and his wife, Jenny, had been frequently attacked by demonic forces while writing a chapter on the occult for a book he was putting together called *The Dust of Death*. I sat quietly and listened. I had arrived with so many questions to ask him but now my mind was blank. I couldn't say anything at all. I could hardly even focus on what he was saying.

My face probably looked as blank as I felt at that moment because Os looked at me rather curiously and said, "Ah, maybe it would be more helpful for you to listen to a couple of my tapes before we talk further.

Play the one called "The East, No Exit" first, then listen to "Encircling Eyes." They're in the library. I'm going to be away for two days, but I'll be back Thursday night. If you have any questions, come by Friday morning, OK? Meanwhile be sure you keep in touch with Birdie."

"The East, No Exit"[1] was the first discussion concerning the philosophical dilemmas of Eastern philosophy versus the Christian alternative that actually made sense to me. While I had always believed that Hinduism and Christianity were fully compatible, (Swami Vivekenanda (1863-1902) had said, "We accept all religions as true"), Os emphasized that far from compatible the two philosophies were radically opposed to one another in their basic concepts of God, reality, morality, and personality. He pointed out that although several gurus taught that the teachings of "the Blessed Lord Jesus Christ" dovetailed perfectly with Hinduism, their claim lacked scholastic integrity. These gurus, Os continued, lifted phrases such as "The Kingdom of Heaven is within you" out of context and blatantly ignored other less pliable statements such as "I am the way, and the truth, and the life; no one comes to the Father, but by me" (John 14:6 RSV). This point especially caught my attention as this had been one of the sayings of Jesus with which I myself had long struggled and had sought to explain away. It was too intolerant a statement, too narrow-minded to possibly be anything other than a misinterpretation or mistranslation of the Bible. Yet the first Epistle and Gospel of John were filled with such statements:

"And the witness is this, that God has given us eternal life, and this life is in His Son. He who has the Son has the life; he who does not have the Son of

[1] Guinness, Os, *The Dust of Death*; (Intervarsity Press), "East, No Exit," p. 49

God does not have the life" (1 John 5:11,12 NASB).

". . . And he [the Holy Spirit], when He comes, will convict the world concerning sin, and righteousness and judgment; concerning sin, because they do not believe in Me" (John 16:8,9 NASB).

". . . For this is the will of My Father, that every one who beholds the Son, and believes in Him, may have eternal life; and I Myself will raise Him up on the last day" (John 6:40 NASB).

"I said therefore to you, that you shall die in your sins; for unless you believe that I am He you shall die in your sins" (John 8:24 NASB).

It was certainly evident that Jesus' contemporaries understood the exclusivity of His claims. "For this cause therefore the Jews were seeking all the more to kill Him, because He not only was breaking the Sabbath, but also was calling God His own Father, making Himself equal with God" (John 5:18 NASB).

Os summarized his discussion by saying: "It is quite plain that, if treated fairly on its own premises, Christianity excludes the full truth and final validity of other religions. If Christianity is true, Hinduism cannot be true in the sense it claims. Even though on the surface it appears that Hinduism is more tolerant, both finally demand an ultimate choice"[2]

Intellectually, Os's discussion made sense to me. Spiritually, however, I couldn't accept it.

It was as if there was a vast insurmountable barrier which was keeping me from taking hold. Suddenly, desperately, all I wanted to do was go home. It was too much. However much sense Os made in that tape or John in his Gospel, I simply couldn't accept it. I felt

[2] *The Dust of Death*, p.50

torn between two powerful relentless forces. The pressure finally drove me to my knees.

I again challenged God to once and for all show me the truth. Was Jesus the greatest avatar, the way-shower; or perhaps the greatest creation of Father God; or was He God uniquely incarnate in human flesh who died to take my sin, as the Gospel of John and Os and Birdie and Kim claimed? Was Pachita working in the power of God or was her source satanic?

"If you can, God, show me now. I'm willing to give up Pachita and yoga and all the rest if I'm wrong. But if not, then I'm putting all this nonsense aside and going on with it at Pachita's. Oh God, let me see the truth!" I had no idea how literally God would answer that prayer.

❀

The night of November, 15, 1972 was damp and cold as I walked alone on the slippery path to Birdie's chalet. It had been drizzling earlier that evening but the clouds were lifting now and I could see a few stars peeping through. Well, maybe with luck it would snow before I left, I thought with a smile. Yesterday I had just about decided to take the next train out of Switzerland, but had changed my mind that morning. I couldn't go until I had some answers. So, perhaps, there would still be time to see it snow after all.

I stopped. A dense black fog was forming all around me, blotting out the path. Within seconds I could see nothing. The dark mist was swirling, alive, filled with the presence of something more monstrous than anything I had ever before encountered. Voices began whispering, hissing incoherent words and laughter in my right ear. An ice-cold breath touched the back of my neck under my hair.

"Hermanito, help me!" I gasped. The voices

shrieked in hideous laughter.

"We're going to kill you!"

I panicked and broke into a run. Something like a giant fist slammed into my back between my shoulders. I pitched forward in the thick darkness and instinctively reached out to break my fall. My fingers found the branch of a small bush and clung to it. I tried to scream out "Jesus!" but an iron hand closed upon my throat choking off the word. All I could do was scream in my mind "Jesus, Jesus, help me!" "He can't help you," the voices shrieked. "He can't help you!"

But then suddenly the grip around my throat loosened—the blackness lifted. I could again see the light of Birdie's chalet at the end of the path.

Birdie's eyes widened a little as I burst into the room. "What on earth is the matter with you!" she exclaimed. "I don't know Birdie," I said, still shaking, "but I'm terrified."

Birdie hurried me into her little prayer room and closed the door. She took my hands in hers and began praying. I tried to focus on her words, but suddenly they sounded so far away. I felt dizzy. My eyes opened. The room seemed to have been taken up in a giant slow-motion whirlwind, spinning slowly round and around. The sound of voices began to build again. I turned my head towards the dark window on my left and froze. Outside I could see the faces of countless demons, contorted, twisted in indescribable rage.

"What is it, Johanna?" Birdie's voice was muffled as though it were coming across a vast distance.

"Can't you see them, Birdie," I gasped, "Can't you see their faces?"

"No," I heard her voice say, "but I know One who can. Satan, in the Name of Jesus Christ of Nazareth, I command you to be gone! I forbid your presence here. I claim the protection of the blood of Jesus upon us.

Go where Jesus sends you!"

Instantly the faces vanished. The room stopped spinning and was filled with a peace beyond all my understanding. They were gone.

I knew what had happened was a direct answer to my prayer. God had literally let me see the source behind my practices. Murderous demonic rage had been the spirits' reaction to my potential decision to accept Jesus Christ of Nazareth *as He is*, rather than as I had come to think He should be. The difference had been subtle, but vast nonetheless. There were still so many things I didn't understand, so many unanswered questions, but I knew beyond any doubt that I had been wrong about Jesus.

I wanted to pray right then to recommit my life to Him on His terms, but Birdie hesitated. She said I should wait until Os could be with us. Perhaps, understandably, she thought I was possessed and that she would need the presence of another strong Christian to help wage the war. There was no question I was severely oppressed, but the demons had never taken possession of me. ("There is a greater Spirit looking over you," Hermanito had said once. His bitter tone now made sense to me.)

I spent most of that night and the next day praying and reading the Bible. Tuesday night, however, the attack came again. I wanted to listen to Os's tape called "Encircling Eyes" before meeting with him and Birdie the next morning. The tape had run only a few minutes when the dense blackness filled the room and fear pressed in on me from all sides with frozen hands. Again my throat was taken in a vise as I tried to call on Jesus. I forced my body to stand and went into the next room, my eyes wide with terror yet unable to say a word to the girls who sat there. They urged me to call Birdie, but when she answered the phone all I could say was her name.

"They're back, aren't they," she said. "I have a terrible emergency here, a suicide threat, but I felt God wanted me to pray for you about twenty minutes ago. Claim the protection of the blood of Jesus, Johanna. Resist them. Is there anyone with you?"

"Yes"—the word came hard. The hand was still on my throat.

"Have them pray with you. I will call you again as soon as I can."

The girls prayed for me. After a while I was able to claim the Lord's protection for myself. By the time Birdie called back the oppression had lifted.

That next morning, Friday, November 17, 1972, at ten a.m. Os and Birdie supported me in prayer as I renounced my involvement with the occult and committed myself to Jesus Christ as my Lord and Savior. I would never again face the darkness alone.

14
New Foundation

"That's the most ridiculous thing I've ever heard!" my father exclaimed. "You've worked with Mind Control and Pachita for over a year. You were 100% convinced it was all God's work. You even got me believing it! Now you want to give it all up because of some experience on a mountain! I just can't believe it, Jo. How many times have I said to you and Kim you've got to keep an open mind. Can't you see the pattern? First you dropped the piano and guitar, then you dropped our church, next the theater. Now *this*. You simply cannot go jumping from one thing to another all your life!" Papa, quite clearly, was exasperated.

It was strange he should feel this way about it, especially since he too had felt an awful evil follow us home in our car sometimes after a meeting at Pachita's—a force that impressed images on our minds of driving ourselves over a cliff to our death. The thing had even possessed my kitten once when she was with us. How could he want me to go back!

"Well, I don't know. Maybe he's got a point," I thought uncomfortably. I wished Os or Birdie were there to talk it over with, but they were thousands of miles away in Switzerland. I knew of no one in Cuernavaca to whom I could go for counsel. Everything had become so confused these past weeks since I had been home. I knew I couldn't go back to Pachita's. The memory of that night on the mountain was too vivid. But maybe I had been hasty in discarding Mind Control. Nothing definite had been said about it at L'Abri. Perhaps, except for the counselors, it was just a neutral technique. I wouldn't summon them, I decided. I would read the cases on my own. I went back into the group.

The results were quite surprising. The accuracy and amount of information I was perceiving psychically astonished even me. It was as though my channels had been tuned and expanded. I was stunned by the implications. Could it be this psychic power, perhaps even Pachita's, was sanctioned by God after all? Perhaps I had misinterpreted what had happened at L'Abri. God had unquestionably shown me the true identity of His Son. I now accepted that with my whole heart. But what if I were mistaken in my conclusion that all the rest was demonic? Surely, God wouldn't allow me to read cases and read them so successfully if it weren't from Him. I always placed myself under His protection before I worked on a case now; I used every opportunity to witness for Jesus. I knew full well the reality and force of His presence, for each time I called upon His name the demons who still pursued me were forced to flee. The attacks were frequent and severe, but I knew the Master was with me and would protect me. Surely He wouldn't let me be deceived again. Yet during the next months the joyous freedom of worship and communion with God which I had experienced at L'Abri was fading.

Desperately I searched through the Bible hoping to find answers. Were my psychic readings and Pachita's work from God or was I again being drawn in by the beautiful side of evil?

One by one verses leaped before me: Deuteronomy 18, Leviticus 20, Exodus 22[1]. The words were clear, and yet somehow these passages threw me into deeper confusion. I decided to find someone with the gift of discerning of spirits to settle the matter once and for all. A friend with whom I still practiced Hatha yoga suggested I talk to someone she knew, a Catholic priest, who in turn directed me to Padre Navarro at a Catholic Center in Mexico City. I went to see him on March 15, 1973.

✺

"That is a difficult question you ask me about this Pachita," Padre Navarro said, his pleasant face wrinkled in a frown. "I don't know the answer, nor do I know of anyone who definitely has discernment in these things. But perhaps God will directly give you the knowledge you ask for. Tell me, has anyone ever laid hands on you that the Spirit of God would be manifested in your life?"

---

[1] "When you enter the land which the Lord your God gives you, you shall not learn to imitate the detestable things of those nations.

"There shall not be found among you anyone who makes his son or his daughter pass through the fire, one who uses divination, one who practices witchcraft, or one who interprets omens, or a sorcerer, or one who casts a spell, or a medium, or a spiritist, or one who calls up the dead.

"For whoever does these things is detestable to the Lord; and because of these detestable things the Lord your God will drive them out before you.

"You shall be blameless before the Lord your God.

"For those nations which you shall disposses, listen to those who practice witchcraft and to diviners, but as for you, the Lord your God has not allowed you to do so" (Deuteronomy 18:9-14 NASB).

"As for the person who turns to mediums and to spiritists, to play the harlot after them, I will also set My face against that person and will cut him off from among his people" (Leviticus 20:6 NASB).

"As for a man or a woman, if there is a medium or a spiritist among them, they shall surely be put to death" (Leviticus 20:27 NASB).

"You shall not allow a sorceress to live" (Exodus 22:18 NASB).

"No, Padre," I replied, "but I would like you to if you will. I want anything that will bring me closer to God." Padre nodded, stood before me and placed both hands upon my head. He prayed for God's protection and mercy upon me. He asked the Holy Spirit to free me and control me; to manifest His fruit in my life.

"Lift your hands to Him, Johanna. It may be He will grant you a special gift—if you hear any words or syllables in your mind, don't be afraid. Speak them to God's glory." As he prayed, I felt a rushing warmth come over me. My mind indeed was filled with strange, beautiful words I have never heard before. Shyly, hesitantly, I spoke a few words, then stopped. I could say no more.

Several days later, however, as I was worshiping the Lord, I felt something break within me and a flood of words and hymns not known to me poured forth in joyous praise of God. It was during a time of prayer shortly after this that it occured to me to test the spirits according to I John 4:1. I went into my laboratory and summoned my counselors.

"You are not the Jesus in the Bible, are you," I challenged the figure of "Jesus" which stood before me in the shadows. There was no reply. His eyes were closed. Mamacita stood close by him. "Then I command you, in the Name of Jesus Christ of Nazareth, tell me: Do you believe that Jesus Christ is God uniquely incarnate in human flesh?" A violent flash—as though from a powerful bomb, brought the walls of my amethyst and gold laboratory down all around me. When I looked up, my counselors had vanished. Again I looked at the words of Deuteronomy and Leviticus. The question was finally settled. The works of a medium were abominations before God. Neither the psychic perceptions of Mind Control nor Pachita's work had its source in God.

Some time later I decided to apply the same test to the gift of the Holy Spirit. I had seen and heard Pachita speak in an unknown tongue many times while under the control of Hermanito, so it obviously was not an exclusive manifestation of the Holy Spirit. I had been deceived before. I recognized it was also possible my "new language" was nothing but a psychological manifestation. I remembered the "language" invented during acting exercises years before. If this were the case, it would probably fade on its own as my theater gibberish had. But, if my gift of "languages" was truly from the Lord, then it would stand the test. I came before the Lord in prayer and worship and told Him I wanted no gift, no ability that was not from Him. I asked Him to take away any psychic ability I might still possess, including the gift of languages, if it fell into that category. Then I said out loud "In Jesus' name, tell me, Is this spirit of tongues within me in submission to the Lordship of Jesus of Nazareth?" Everything within me cried out "YES!" in a burst of overwhelming joy. Had it not, I would have renounced my gift as one more subtle lie from the enemy.

Padre Navarro nodded approvingly as I related all this to him. "What you have done is good. Any true gift from God will stand the test. Now, have you brought your occultic books and artifacts for me as I asked you?" I nodded.

"Good! Be sure none of these things remains in your house. They can become focal points for the demons. I will see to it that these are destroyed by fire."

❀

June of 1973 proved to be yet another turning point. Campus Crusade for Christ was giving a six week intensive training course in the Bible. Despite an aversion to what then seemed to me a mechanical presentation of the gospel on their part, I decided to apply. It was one of the best decisions of my life. Not only did their courses give me the basic tools I needed to begin a systematic study of the Bible, but I found, if only for a few weeks, the fellowship I desperatly needed. One teacher in particular, Warren Willis, and his wife, Diane, gave so freely of themselves to me. Their teaching, love, and concern was a source of tremendous encouragement. There was one other family who reached out to help me over the rugged terrain of those early days; Swede and Judy Anderson, who headed the Latin American outreach of Campus Crusade back then. Their three children, Valerie, Tiffany, and Matthew, were my special "cuddle-bunnies" and brought a great deal of laughter and fellowship to my life.

Two important things came from those six weeks with Campus Crusade. First, I began to ascertain that I had not, after all, committed some exquisite form of intellectual suicide in my embrace of Scripture as the revelation of absolute truth.

The second was meeting Dr. Walter Martin. Dr. Martin was there lecturing on the cults and the occult. He and three of his children, Brian, Danny and Jill, bravely risked life and limb in my old black Ford while I happily dragged them up and down the countryside under the cover of "tour guide."

It was at Walter's suggestion that I sifted through a depressing stack of my diaries, notes, and calendars in order to record the material for this book on tape. This project was undertaken about the time I almost was because of my third case of hepatitis. The resulting tapes were therefore not altogether complete or coherent, but the transcript Walter made from them has since proved invaluable.

Walter was also indirectly reponsible for the direction my life had taken. He met Kim at a lecture he was giving in Oklahoma around October of 1973. She was just back from Europe and wasn't sure where she wanted to go next. He suggested she stop at the Light and Power House, then a small Bible school which had been started by Hal Lindsey and a group of men out of Dallas Seminary. The House was located near the UCLA campus in Westwood, California. She went and soon wrote to suggest that I apply as well. I waited for a year before doing so; I still hadn't quite finished wreaking havoc with my father's real estate business. When the four of us finally had it (Dad, Mom, the business, and I), I applied to the Light and Power House and was accepted for a Fall term of 1974.

While managing to remain comparatively undistinguished in the intellectual arena of biblical scholastics, I did learn a good deal. The deeper I went into the study of salvation history, textual criticism and analysis, systematic theology and prophecy, the more awed I became at the solid, objective basis there was for my faith.

God also used the time to begin teaching me lessons on another level as well, which made the two years I spent as a student at the Light and Power House very trying in some ways. My background of committed isolationism and an aura of general weirdness which seemed to cling to me like the vague odor of sulphur complicated the relatively unfamiliar task of building friendships. Also, my unabashed affection and concern for the welfare of stray kitties marked me as "psychologically unstable" to some and, in one circle not closely allied to the school's philosophy on the subject, "possessed by a demon of cats."

It was true that over the years I had come to love and trust cats considerably more than I did humans. Certainly cats can be aloof and unresponsive if raised by people who expect that from them. But for me, they were challenging and delightfully furry little friends. I understood them and respected them. They, in turn, responded to me with a warmth of affection usually associated with dogs. Given a choice, I usually preferred their company to that of most people I knew.

All this is to say that I was not considered highly eligible dating material in the Christian circles I now frequented. I did eventually develop several close supportive friendships with a few brothers of the House, but in the four and one half years since Beck, I had not dated more than five or six times. There were times when it was lonely, but I had come to terms with loneliness.

"It's in the Lord's hands," I answered when asked about my feelings on the subject at a House meeting one day. "I would enjoy dating more than I do, I'll admit, but several weeks ago I decided that if God chooses to keep me single for the rest of my life, it's fine with me. There are a lot of advantages to being uncommitted, you know. Actually, I *like* being single. In any case, God knows how I can best serve Him." I meant it.

Exactly two weeks after this pronouncement, on Monday April 19, 1976, I met Randolph.

❀

In a way, Randolph became a Christian as a result of his cancer. He already had two operations for the melanoma on his shoulder. The malignancy had invaded his lymphatic system; he was not expected to survive.

The news hit hard. His mother had died of cancer when he was seventeen. But then, after several days of struggle, he decided he wasn't going to let it get him down. He was determined to enjoy what time he had left. So, he went sailing in the Caribbean, surfing in Malibu, and spent days on Hawaiian beaches stringing puka shells with his children. He had come to terms with death.

Over the next year, however, his prognosis changed; there was a good chance he would survive after all. It was good news, but his reaction to it caught him by surprise. He should have been elated. He loved his life. Despite a broken marriage, it had been full of excitement and adventure. He had travelled all over the world, patented several inventions, run his own diving company, and, as a marine engineer, had worked on the Glomar Explorer project. Yet now, when confronted with the prospect of going back into his life as it had been, he felt a vague sense of disappointment. It suddenly seemed so empty.

It was at that point he decided to seriously evaluate God to see what, if anything, He had to say for Himself. After months of analyzing, reading and praying, along with a series of amazing circumstances that can only be ascribed to the hand of God, Randolph accepted the Lord as his Savior in August of 1975.

Eight months later, we met at the Light and Power House during a special series of lectures that Hal Lindsey was giving on the philosophy of ministry.

Randolph had been invited to attend the lectures by a teacher who wasn't at all sure why he was asking him to go, except that he had a feeling that God had something for him there that day. For better or worse He did: Me. We were married in a beautiful candlelight wedding six months and three days later.

Our home for the next three-and-a-half years was on wheels and was exactly twenty-four feet long from end to end. We dubbed it "The Ark" and soon learned to maneuver the tiny apartment with all the choreographed grace of ballerinas. We were so alike in our interests and personalities that the limitations of our space merely served to bind us all the more closely in fellowship and love. We shared everything—books, a bizarre sense of humor, a love of classical music and kitty cats, our thoughts . . .which didn't always see eye to eye and which occasionally led to lively altercations. We learned new interests from each other as well; I learned to Boogie board in the Malibu surf (I'm told I'm quite a sight in my fins and wetsuit), and Randolph went with me to museums. (He has also learned how to cook, iron, vacuum and wash dishes.)

Most of all, we shared our love for the Lord. Over a period of months it became increasingly clear to us that Randolph had a calling for the ministry. He applied and was accepted for the fall term of 1977 at Christian Associates Seminary, which at one time had been the Light and Power House.

We value those years of study beyond any other thing we could have done. We knew that time in seminary would not only give Randolph the tools needed for ministry, but would also strengthen our relationship with the Lord and with each other. I was able to audit the classes with him for the first year, and between that and typing all his papers, was able to build on what I had learned at the House.

❊

Two years later we moved from the Ark to a little apartment. As I sit here in the warm California sun looking at the flowers in my garden the years of terror and Pachita seem so remote. The spiritual attacks and depressions which had been so intense even during my stay at the Light and Power House decreased as Randolph and I spent time in daily prayer. God has taught me so much about His grace and unconditional love and acceptance through this man He has given me as my covering.

Then when we joined the Vineyard Christian Fellowship in West Los Angeles, a whole new dimension of worship and fellowship was added to our lives.

But growth is a process. There have been times—many of them—when I have come to a standstill and allowed the enemy to pummel me for a season before I even was aware of what was happening. It takes time to be transformed through the renewing of the mind.

As for Pachita, I was never to see her again. She died in April of 1979.

15
Velvet Claws

I have not written this story as an exercise in narcissistic morbidity. Writing the account of my life—reliving those days of darkness—has been one of the most difficult things I have ever done. Those of you with occult histories of your own will know what I mean. Nor have I written my story to glorify the deeds of darkness. Should anyone come away from this book with the idea that I am condoning such action, I would wonder whether he had read carefully what I have said. I have shared my story because of the times in which we live.

I realize that the words I am about to share with you may seem harsh, perhaps even (God forbid!) preachy to some. I sincerely ask your forgiveness if that proves to be the case. And yet, before the Lord, I cannot apologize for what I am about to say in the following chapters, for I believe with all my heart it is the truth.

Those of you who are—or have been—in the occult, and are seeking a way out of the darkness, or those of you who have friends or loved ones still under bondage, will understand the relevance of my story. In the last two chapters of this book I have shared some of the basic principles I have learned from many years of hard study and personal experience concerning the discernment of false prophets and healers and the means of freedom from occultic bondage. I pray these chapters will be of help and encouragement to you.

But there are many others of you who have never had, or been aware of having had, any personal involvement with the occult and may be wondering what on earth this story has to do with you.

Everything!

The occult is not a passing fad. It is here and will continue to grow and spread like a mass of suffocating jungle vines until the promised return of Jesus Christ.

I think most of us would get a nasty shock if it were possible to take an honest inventory of those among our friends, co-workers, even church members, who are or have been involved in the occult or have had occult experiences. Because of a prevailing attitude of unbelief and ridicule found in many places, most have simply remained underground and kept these things to themselves. My story, for the most part, is actually quite common among occultists.

If you believe you have never encountered the occult before, perhaps it is because you have not recognized it as such. Occult practices are frequently disguised as the most innocent, even time-honored, of pastimes.

I've lost count of how many individuals, even while under severe demonic bondage, have said to me, "Oh, but I've never been involved in the occult! I just played around with the Ouija board a few times!" (or astrology, or tea-leaf reading, or rod-and-pendulum, or Dungeons and Dragons, or seances, or palmistry, or tarot cards, etc.)

That, perhaps, is analogous to saying "Oh, I'm not really pregnant! Just a couple of months' worth." The effects may not show up much in your life right at the moment, but chances are they will down the line.

We can no longer afford to ignore what is happening around us. We are living in the end times, and the threefold warning given by our Lord has come to pass with a vengeance: false messiahs and false prophets abound; the flock is being swept by every wind of doctrine and the spirits of devils are working miracles as never before since Jesus walked the earth (Matthew 24:4, 11, 24; Mark 13:4-6; 21,22). If you have not been aware of it before now, you will be.

Softening Our Defenses

The world is being carefully groomed for the arrival of the one whom Scripture calls "the man of lawlessness . . . the son of destruction" (II Thessalonians 2:3), "that is, the one whose coming is in accord with the activity of Satan, with all *power* and *signs* and *false wonders*," (II Thessalonians 2:9)—the Antichrist. I believe this man is in the world today and Satan is working overtime to prepare mankind to hail the satanic signs and miracles he will perform (Revelation 13:13) as being wonders from the hand of God Himself.

You've seen it.

Television talk-show hosts are falling over one another to get the latest psychic wonder to appear for an interview. I watched an "extraterrestrial master" perform psychic surgery on the Bionic Woman. For well over a decade we have laughed at the cute antics of Samantha, the "good" witch on *Bewitched*, and Jeanie, the genie-in-the-bottle in *I Dream of Jeanie*. After-school specials and stories for the children are filled with tales of ghosts and goblins and of good little girls and boys learning to become witches and wizards. From Casper the Ghost to cartoons of space-age marvels children are being taught to accept supernatural phenomena as a wonderful part of their every-day life to be joyfully and fearlessly embraced!

Ouija boards are sold in almost every toy store—frequently next to "Dungeons and Dragons," a game which is occultic to the core, whatever its devotees may believe. There is hardly a paper in this country that does not publish a daily horoscope. Weekly publications such as the *Enquirer* and the *Star*, among half a dozen others all over the country, are filled with the latest psychic information and predictions. The pilot for a new television serial called "Phoenix" gives us an extraterrestrial shaman and "messiah" upon whom the salvation of the world may depend. He is endowed with awesome psychic powers, not the least of which are levitation, psychokinesis and acute ESP. Literally dozens of music groups with openly declared satanic ties (just look at the album covers and titles sometime!) flood the market. Some even proclaim their praises to their Lord Satan in backward masquing of their records.

Eastern gurus have flooded the market with transcendental euphoria. Their doctrines of karma and reincarnation . . . radically tailored for Western mass market consumption, of course . . . have been embraced by millions. Yoga classes abound. Courses in TM and witchcraft and parapsychology are being offered for credit at numerous major institutions, not to mention high schools. In fact, one school system I know of—doubtless there are many more—has included reading material on the supernatural for its fourth, fifth and sixth graders on the excuse that the subject is of great interest to the children.

Titles of these "high interest books"[1] include: *Witches; Ghosts and Ghouls; Secrets of the Great Magi-*

---

[1]*Orange Cherry Media*—1981-1982 Catalog for grades K-8, p. 5. Orange Cherry Media, 7 Delano Drive, Bedford Hills, New York 10507

*cians; Palm Reading; Spells, Chants and Potions.*The titles of accompanying filmstrips in this series are equally revealing: *Magic and Witchcraft* which "explores the world of magic and the supernatural . . . witches and folk tales;" *The Signs of Astrology,* "an easy-to-understand description of the signs of the Zodiac." This captivating filmstrip shows how astrologists try to foretell human events by studying the stars. The third filmstrip in this series is called *Foretelling the Future* which "examines the practice of fortune telling through palmistry, crystal balls, and tarot cards." This is followed by *Powers of the Mind*—a "fascinating look at those who claim extrasensory or unusual mental powers."

Well-meaning, capable educators may indeed be teaching children how to read with these "High Interest/Low Reading Level" series, but they are inadvertently bringing spiritual disaster into the lives of countless thousands of our children.

But then it is the children who are now the primary target of Satan's pre-evangelistic campaign. Their young minds are more easily molded and programmed to accept the reality of the supernatural.

The *Calendar* section of the *Los Angeles Times* featured a fascinating review by Michael London of Steven Spielberg's movie "E.T. the Extra-Terrestrial."

Eight "veterans" of so-called "UFO experiences" were invited to a special screening of "E.T." Some of their comments during the group discussion following the showing and subsequent phone calls with Mr. London are indicative of a growing awareness of at least part of the actual purpose of such films and the phenomena they deal with.

"This is a true movie, not a romance," said one. "It's part of a conditioning process to prepare us for the arrival of alien beings."

"The movie is a vehicle," said another. "A lot of it is

hokey, but it also invites the audience to be less afraid of the so-called paranormal. *And what better place to start than with the children.*"

The list of examples could go on and on. The countries of Europe, Africa, Asia and Latin America could make their own extensive lists.

Since the mid 1960's we have been hit with a veritable deluge of occult information and phenomena. Did you know that there are at least sixty-five million people involved in some form of occult practice, ranging from tarot cards and Ouija boards to astrology, spiritualism and outright Satan worship? (In light of some of *their* experiences, my story is not as "hopelessly weird" as some may have thought.) Over thirty million people are involved in the cults.

And yet in the years I have been lecturing on this subject, it is frightening to me how many believers, even pastors, are totally ignorant about these schemes of the devil and the disastrous impact occult practices are having within the church.

Faithless Shepherds

C.S. Lewis is known for, among other things, a poignantly accurate, if admittedly overused, quotation from his *Screwtape Letters*:

> There are two equal and opposite errors into which our race can fall about devils. One is to disbelieve in their existence. The other is to believe and to feel an excessive and unhealthy interest in them. They themselves are equally pleased by both errors and hail a materialist or a magician with the same delight.[1]

---

[1] Lewis, C.S., *Screwtape Letters* (New York: MacMillan Co., 1964-67).

There are clear examples of both these extremes, along with numerous fascinating variations, to be found within the body today. Under the tutelage of Bultmann and the neo-orthodox and liberal theologians, many, including pastors, no longer believe in a personal Satan at all, much less in the possibility of genuine satanic phenomena. The "unsophisticated," "unscientific" accounts in Scripture of Satan and demons have proved an embarrassment to them, but then so have the miracles of Jesus, His deity, His virgin birth, His death on a cross for our redemption, His bodily resurrection, and the doctrine of the Trinity. The fact that Scripture records that Jesus had a face-to-face confrontation with Satan is merely taken as evidence that Jesus was a well-intentioned, highly shrewd and intelligent but naive child of His times. He was either bowing to the beliefs of the day, or hallucinating something awful due to an acute state of vitamin deficiency caused by his forty-day fast, as the late Bishop James Pike suggests.[2]

It is from the very pulpits of our nation that the truth and power of the Word of God has been stripped naked, leaving the flock with a pathetic, milk-sop caricature of Jesus. They have been left "holding to a form of godliness, although they have denied its power . . ." (II Timothy 3:5). And we are then amazed because our children turn to drugs, cults, and the occult to fill the vacuum in their lives.

But, in the wake of the Bishop James Pike, a new trend has developed among these "shepherds." While scorning the concept of a personal Satan and his host of demons, they have embraced the field of

[2] Pike, Bishop James A., *The Other Side*, (Doubleday & Company, Inc., 1968), p. 147.

parapsychology.[3] The supernatural manifestations of God seen in Scripture are ascribed to the work of powerful mediums and psychics, of whom they believe Jesus was foremost.

The Wisdom of Men

The injunctions in the Old Testament against consulting mediums, such as Leviticus 19:31, are dismissed as the words of "Jewish religious professionals—the priests and prophets"—who "had to protect their own roles as those who could reveal and interpret the Word of God, so they were quick to denounce with vehemence any competitors, like mediums and foretellers of the future. In this regard, those scriptural injunctions are of little help to us today, for our world view is so different."[4]

In other words, according to the Bishop, the term "Word of God" in reference to the Scriptures was nothing but a figure of speech. For him, the Bible was not the revelation of Absolute Truth, given by the Living God, but rather the writings of frightened, insecure men who were desperately seeking to protect their jobs and status.[5] Having rejected the testimony of Scripture, he left himself adrift, with only *his experience* left to define and mold his world view. "My *experiences*

---

[3]   *Parapsychology*—"The study and investigation of psychic phenomena, such as telepathy, clairvoyance and extrasensory perception." It is informally known as "psi phenomena." (New Webster's Dictionary).

Because parapsychology is now a "science," many assume it therefore has nothing to do either with demons or the injunctions of Scripture against their pursuit. One does not necessarily need to believe in demons or spirits of any kind, for that matter, in order to be involved in the occult.

[4]   Pike, *The Other Side,* p. 284.

[5]   For further discussion on the subject of Scriptural reliability see *The New Testament Documents: Are They Reliable?* by F.F. Bruce, (InterVarsity Press, Downers Grove, Il).

with psi phenomena, as well as the extensive study that they have stimulated, have led me to be even more open to and to affirm tentatively an understanding of man and his universe that seems *more adequate* [italics mine] than the conventional Christian one or that of its near relative, Western secularism."[6] And what was the ultimate revelation of that experience? It came during one of the Bishop's last seances with the medium Ena Twigg. A spirit who claimed to be Jim, Jr. spoke through the medium and, in answer to the Bishop's question, "Have you heard anything over there about Jesus, or a Jesus?" answered:

> Oh, it is difficult, I'm afraid I might hurt you. I might hurt you . . . They talk about him—a mystic, a seer, yes, a seer. Oh, but, Dad, they don't talk about him as a savior. As an example, you see? . . . You see, I want to tell you, I would like to tell you, Jesus is triumphant, you know? But it's not like that. I don't understand it yet. I may, sometime I may . . . You don't want me to tell you what I don't know . . . not a savior, that's the important thing—an example . . . Don't you ever believe that God can be personalized. He is the Central Force, and you all give your quota toward it. Do you agree with me, Dad?[7]

He did. And that belief led him to his eventual destruction. The words of I John 2:22-23 would have been meaningless to him—as they are to so many of those who "went out from us but were not really of us" (I John 2:19). "Who is the liar but the one who denies that Jesus is the Christ? This is the antichrist, the one who denies the Father and the Son. Whoever denies the Son does not have the Father . . . These things I have written to you concerning those who are trying to deceive you" (I John 2:22, 23, 26).

---

6   Pike, *The Other Side*, p. 373.

7   Pike, *The Other Side*, p. 383.

"Professing to be wise, they became fools."
(Romans 1:22).

The "Ostrich" Syndrome

Others, while believing in Jesus and the person of
Satan, ascribe just about every form of occultism not to
the "scientific" manifestations of parapsychology, or to
"departed spirits" working through mediums, or, for
that matter, to demonic intervention, but rather to
sleight of hand or to some psychological aberration.

It is unquestionably true that for every one hundred
"occultic manifestations," most are fraudulent. Bogus
palm readers, astrologers, psychics, mediums and occultists of every description certainly abound. Their
"manifestations" can indeed frequently be duplicated
by those proficient in *legerdemain*. These skilled magicians argue that, because they can reproduce much of
the phenomena by sleight of hand and psychologically
analyze the rest, *all* such phenomena are therefore unquestionably fraudulent. So, it is concluded, because
these things don't exist, believers need not be in fear of
them. In one sense, people who have taken this position are correct: We need have no fear whatever of the
frauds.

But, unfortunately, because many occultists have
been proven fraudulent does not automatically prove
they all are. The existence of the counterfeit by defini-
tion must presuppose the existence of the original.
Without it, a counterfeit is meaningless.

Demonic Wonders

To assert that demons do not work miracles, that no
medium can indeed receive manifestations of a supernatural nature, one must wreak awful havoc with the
testimony of both the Old and New Testaments. From
Genesis to Revelation God speaks of a powerful being

whom He calls Satan and continually warns us against him and his awesome, malevolent, seductive power.

We see the magicians of Pharaoh reproducing the signs God gave through Moses, doing "the same with their secret arts," turning their staffs to serpents, turning the waters of Egypt to blood, causing frogs to cover the land. These are impressive tricks for "mere frauds." But there came a point when they could not counterfeit God's plague of lice, (despite the fact that I always thought lice were from the pit of hell and Satan's own). Their failure forced them to admit "This is the finger of God" (Exodus 8:19).

In Deuteronomy 13 we are warned concerning "a prophet or a dreamer of dreams" who arises among the people and "gives you a sign or a wonder, and the sign or the wonder comes true concerning which he spoke to you, saying 'Let us go after other gods (whom you have not known) and let us serve them,' you shall not listen to the words of that prophet or that dreamer of dreams; for the Lord your God is testing you . . ." (Deuteronomy 13:1-3).

These terms, the Hebrew aoth, which means "signs," and moteth, which is the word for wonders, translated by Old Testament scholars in the Septuagint around 250 B.C., are the same words used by Jesus in Matthew 24:24: "For false Christs and false prophets will arise and will show great signs and wonders . . ." The word aoth translates as the Greek semeion (signs), and the word moteth is teras (wonders). These are precisely the same terms used to describe the miracles of Jesus in the Gospel accounts. Hal Lindsey tracked these terms down for me. He concludes that whether in reference to demonic miracles or those from the hand of God, these words can in no way be taken to imply fake signs or wonders such as those produced by the skilled magicians of today.

Revelation 16:14 speaks of the "spirits of demons, performing signs," and the Antichrist himself, when he is revealed, will perform "great signs, so that he even makes fire come down out of heaven to the earth in the presence of men" (Revelation 13:13). This is the one "whose coming is in accord with the activity of Satan, with all *power* and *signs* and *false wonders*" (II Thessalonians 2:9).

The meaning of the word "false" in this passage does not imply "fraudulent" in the sense that no true miracle has taken place. These demonic miracles *do* take place. The question that must always be asked is not only *Did a genuine miracle occur?* but also *What is the source behind it?*

In the Scriptures, God performs signs and wonders and miracles to authenticate the words of His prophets and apostles, bearing witness by these to the truth of the gospel of Jesus Christ (Hebrews 2:4). It is with miracles and wonders that the identity of Jesus was confirmed, but these signs were never an end in and of themselves. They were always designed to deepen our understanding and our faith in the Living God and in His Son, and it was that response of faith which Jesus always sought. It was "in order that you may know that the Son of Man has authority on earth to forgive sins" that He said to the paralytic, "I say to you, rise, take up your pallet and go home" (Mark 2:10-11).

Define Your Terms

Today we are seeing many signs and wonders. They may even be done in the name of Jesus and "to the glory of my Father above." But *which Jesus? Which Father?* To use His name does not guarantee its source, for many today have so redefined Him that what they call "Jesus" in no way resembles the Jesus of the Bible,[8] and so they lead the undiscerning into the worship of "other gods whom you have not known."

> For if one comes and preaches *another Jesus* whom we have not preached, or you receive a *different spirit* which you have not received, or a *different gospel* which you have not accepted, *you bear this beautifully (II Corinthians 11:4).*

Incidentally, Paul said this to a church "not lacking in any gift" (I Corinthians 1:7), a church *sincere* in its devotion to the Lord (I Corinthians 1:4-8). Yet their gifting and sincerity alone, Paul says, does not preclude the possibility of their being tricked and deceived and led astray because of their undiscernment, and their unscriptural emphasis on experience.

The Devil Made Me Do It

The second error of which C.S. Lewis spoke concerning demons is "to believe and to feel an excessive and unhealthy interest in them."[9]

He was primarily alluding to the non-believer who, in direct defiance and disobedience to the Word of God (Deuteronomy 18:9-14; Leviticus 20:6,27; 19:31; Isaiah 8:19), has pursued occult, that is, secret or hidden activities.

Occult practices usually have two main objectives: *supernatural knowledge,* usually concerning the future, and *power* (Genesis 3:5), which the occultist seeks to gain through manipulation of supernatural forces and beings. Demons can be most accommodating, and will cheerfully provide this occult knowledge and power, knowing that in seeking, *demanding,* these things outside the confines of the

---

[8] See *Kingdom of the Cults* by Walter Martin, chapter entitled "The Jesus of the Cults."

[9] Lewis, *Screwtape Letters.*

Word of God (Deuteronomy 29:29), the individual places himself in direct violation of the first and second Commandments . . .

> You shall have no other gods before Me. You shall not make for yourself an idol, or any likeness of what is in heaven above or on the earth beneath or in the water under the earth. You shall not worship them or serve them (Exodus 20:3-5a).

To seek power and knowledge from supernatural sources other than God is in every sense to place other gods before Him, and removes that individual from God's protection:

> . . . for I, the Lord your God, am a jealous God, visiting the iniquity of the fathers on the children, on the third and fourth generation of those who hate Me . . . (Exodus 20:5b,5c)

It is a well-known fact among practicing occultists that their powers, their "talent," can be inherited down to the third and fourth generation. Their participation in what God has repeatedly called abomination (Deuteronomy 18:9-14 KJV) gives Satan, the prince of this earth, the legal right to bind them and their descendants unto the third and fourth generation. Frequently, a great-grandchild will not even be aware of his ancestors' involvement until he himself, perhaps, becomes, or tries to become, a believer. Then, quite literally, all hell can break loose for him, though he himself may never have participated in occult practices. He may find it difficult to believe in Jesus, however much he may want to, or come under the kind of demonic attack which I myself was subjected to.

It is at this point where so many believers in our churches today fall into the error of "excessive and unhealthy interest" in demons; not only do they believe in them, but they automatically ascribe *every* possible human flaw, struggle or misfortune to direct demonic intervention.

These brothers unquestionably love the Lord, and the body may well learn from their zeal and dedication. But frequently their zeal is not in accordance with the knowledge of sound scriptural exegesis. To state that *everyone* is "possessed" and in need of deliverance is in stark contradiction to the focus and teachings of Scripture.

Exercise Your Faith

We fight against the world and the flesh as well as the devil. Paul tells us that the deeds of the flesh (Galatians 5:19-21, along with almost two dozen supporting passages) are evident, and time and again he, and every other writer of the New Testament exhorts us to *walk* according to the light (Ephesians 5:8, 15), to *resist* temptation (I Corinthians 10:13), to *quit sinning* (Hebrews 12:4); not to run around superstitiously blaming everything on demons. The focus of Scripture is on *exercising* our faith, not *exorcising* it.

They have built their theology on the quagmire of "experience" and in so doing have unwittingly opened the door for destruction within the church. Untold damage has been done by seeking to exorcise nonexistent demons from epileptic or mentally ill people. The symptoms of these illnesses can frequently appear to be demonic, but the people who feel themselves called to minister in this area have a responsibility before God to understand what the balance of Scripture is on the subject, and to learn the difference between genuine mental illness and the demonic.

Dr. Kurt Koch has two important works which deal with this subject: *Occult Bondage and Deliverance* and *Christian Counseling and Occultism,* both put out by Kregel Publications.

Dr. Koch has ministered for over 40 years in this

field to more than 20,000 people. His books present some of the most helpful and scripturally balanced positions on demonic oppression and deliverance I have yet come across. I don't believe that anyone should venture into counseling those under occult subjection without first giving careful consideration to these works.

16
Genuine Vs. Counterfeit

I am a charismatic. I believe that the gifts of the Holy Spirit, including prophecy, miracles, healing and tongues, are operative within the body today. I have seen many people miraculously healed by the Hand of God through prayer, including my own husband, who was healed overnight when God literally fused together two painful disintegrating vertebrae. I have heard true words of knowledge and tongues and prophecy spoken. *The original does exist.* That is precisely why Satan is busy producing counterfeits to the work of God through psychics and mediums. That is to be expected of him.

In light of the last chapter, we shouldn't be too surprised to find practicing occultists within most of our denominations, including the Catholic church. It is a well known fact that Jean Dixon attends mass every single morning. More than a few of the "miracles" hailed within the Catholic church, such as weeping madonnas, bleeding trees and statues, visions, stigmatta, etc., are distinctly occultic in nature.

Edgar Cayce was a popular Bible teacher.

Even in my own childhood Episcopal church in Mexico, psychic Ruth Montgomery was an honored member. Our church library proudly displayed all her books on Jean Dixon and psychic phenomena.

Church bazaars all over the country have been known to include "gypsy" palm readers as a fund raising gimmick.

What many of us in the church *never* expect is to find satanic counterfeits operating in the very midsts of pentecostal and charismatic meetings. Yet what I have seen happen in some of these meetings has made my blood run cold.

Paul has told us to "desire earnestly spiritual gifts." As the Spirit of God moves among His people, we should expect Him to do wonderful things in our midst. But because of our eagerness to see the power of God at work, because of our hunger to see signs and wonders and miracles, many of us have become undiscerning and have embraced *every* ecstatic vision, *every* supernatural manifestation, as from the hand of God.

How Firm Our Foundation

We have, ever so subtly, allowed our base to shift from the solid objective grounding of God's Word and have come instead to place our focus on our experience as the standard for our beliefs.

In the second Epistle to Timothy, Paul tells the young disciple that "All Scripture is inspired by God and profitable for teaching, for reproof, for correction, for training in righteousness; that the man of God may be adequate, equipped for every good work" (II Timothy 3:16-17. In this context Paul then exhorts Timothy to

Preach the word; be ready in season and out of season; reprove, rebuke, exhort, with great patience and instruction. For the time will come when they *will not endure sound doctrine;* but wanting to have their ears tickled, they will accumulate for themselves teachers in accordance to their own desires; and will turn away their ears from the truth, and will turn aside to myths. (II Timothy 4:2-4)

That is, they will turn aside from the objective revelation of the Word of truth, basing their beliefs instead on their experience, twisting Scripture until it "supports" their opinions.

That first week in college, when the gospel was shared with me, I welcomed it with open arms. I confessed my sins before God and asked Jesus to enter my life as my Lord and Savior. I know, on the basis of God's word, that I was born again, and I received in my spirit the assurance of my salvation. I gave myself to Him with my whole heart.

But I did not understand the importance of carefully, systematically studying His Word. I had no real understanding of *what* I believed or *why* I believed it.[1] And so, in time, I began to build my relationship with God based on my experience. My *experience* told me the healings and miracles I witnessed at Pachita's were of God. My *feelings* assured me the work there was holy, for the name of Jesus was used and there was a crucifix on the altar, and demons were "cast out." Soon my "logic" told me the Bible was too narrow in its view, and, as the work of men, was bound to be filled with error and mistranslation. Ultimately, I came to believe Jesus was *a* way to God—but not *the* Way, *the* Truth, *the* Life. Gently, a step at a time, I fell away from the faith, unwittingly "paying attention to deceitful spirits and doctrines of demons" (I Timothy 4:1).

Because of my ignorance of the Word of God, I became deceived. Ultimately, because I *was* a child of God, because I wanted more than anything else to know the Truth, He delivered me. But because of my

[1] Little, Paul E., *Know What You Believe* (Victor Books, 1970).

immaturity in the Lord and my willful ignorance of His Word, I wandered in the darkness for many years, despite my sincerity.

Sincerely Wrong

Many of us in the church believe our *sincerity* acts as a kind of magical protection against all demonic intrusion and deception. But nowhere in the Bible is there a single verse that assures us our sincerity alone protects us or guarantees us automatic immunity from demonic deception. Not one.

On the contrary. The pages of the New Testament are filled with warning after warning to us to "be of sober spirit, be on the alert" (I Peter 5:8 and Ephesians 6:18); to let no one deceive us with empty words (Ephesians 5:6); nor to allow ourselves to be taken captive "through philosophy and empty deception, according to the tradition of men, according to the elementary principles of the world, rather than according to Christ" (Colossians 2:8).

If we *cannot* be deceived, then why are we told not to believe every spirit, but to "test the spirits to see whether they are from God" (I John 4:1)? Jesus Himself has warned us that "false Christs and false prophets will arise and will show great signs and wonders, so as to mislead, if possible, even the elect" (Matthew 24:24). (Some say here that "if possible" carries the implication that it is not. But the "if" used here in the original Greek is a first class conditional clause which means: "if, and it certainly is possible . . . ", even if only for a season.)

Paul urges us to put on the full armor of God, "that you may be able to stand firm against the schemes of the devil" (Ephesians 6:11), for he was afraid for the church,

> . . . lest as the serpent deceived Eve by his craftiness, your

minds should be led astray from the simplicity and purity of devotion to Christ (II Corinthians 11:3).

I too am afraid for our church, for I have seen a different spirit come among us because of our ignorance and undiscernment concerning the gifts of God and the schemes of the devil.

Please don't misunderstand me here. I believe it is *because the charismatic church is alive* and manifesting the power of God that Satan is seeking to produce his counterfeits in our midst.

My words are not meant in anyway as an attack, but rather as a desperate warning for us to recognize the "wiles of the devil" so that we may be effective witnesses to the holiness and power of God in the last days. As it stands now, many of our churches are in serious danger of occult contamination, and I could not speak of the beautiful side of evil without addressing these excesses within the charismatic church.

Occultic Background

For example, believers with occultic backgrounds which have never been renounced are manifesting mediumistic gifts and techniques which go undiscerned in the atmosphere of ecstatic hoopla which frequently characterizes so many meetings. Some of these believers are often still involved in such things as astrology and palm reading, and usually completely unaware of the spiritual dangers involved. Somewhere down the line, sooner or later, they will experience an emptiness in their walk with God—a strange reluctance to read and trust His Word. A black, lingering depression settles over them, plaguing them with doubts about God and their salvation. In more severe cases, they may come under direct demonic attack, as I did.

These symptoms of demonic oppression can, of course, have very different sources. Not all depressions or doubts are directly satanic in origin. But they inevitably arise in connection with those who have occultic backgrounds. Mediumistic gifts can, but do not always, automatically disappear when one becomes a believer. Mine didn't. I was more psychic than ever when I returned from L'Abri, and from what I've seen in many of our meetings, my abilities would have been acclaimed as the gift of "words of knowledge" and "prophecy." What is *was*, was clairvoyance.

It was not until I took the *offensive* in my on-going battle against Satan, making a *full* list of *all* my sins (some which I had left out at L'Abri), confessing them openly before the Lord, again renouncing them and all the works and gifts of Satan, and then *totally* refraining from practicing these things, that these psychic powers faded over a period of months. It has been so with many others whom I've counseled. I truly believe that those with occultic backgrounds should wait a season before seeking and exercising any of the more "spectacular" gifts of the Spirit until they have matured in the grace *and* knowledge of the Lord.

Paul tells us that it is as a *result* of growing in maturity "to the measure of the stature which belongs to the fullness of Christ . . . " that we will no longer be as children, "tossed here and there by waves, and carried about by every wind of doctrine . . . " (Ephesians 4:13c, 14b); "Solid food is for the mature, who because of practice have their senses *trained* to discern good and evil" (Hebrews 5:14). [Italics mine.]

Tongues

And yet there are so many of us who, in earnestness and love, seek to foist certain gifts, which may have proved a great blessing to us personally, upon every believer, however immature in the Lord, and in complete disregard as to what gifts the *Lord* may have for that person. In so doing I have watched these believers fall into techniques employed by the cults to produce the desired effect.

For example: "Arise upon your feet, speak or make some sound, continue to make sounds of some kind and the Lord will make a tongue or language of it." This was the technique used by Joseph Smith, the founder of Mormonism.[2] I have seen others instructed to "Say 'Praise the Lord!' or 'Our Father who art in heaven' a hundred times in a row as fast as you can. When you begin tripping over the words, just let it go! Praise the Lord, you've got the gift!" This sort of thing is an insult to the Holy Spirit and borders on blasphemy.

More frequently than not, such manifestations are induced by a state of ecstatic self-hypnosis which closely resembles certain forms of clinical neuroses and brain disorders, and which is purely psychological in its effect.

Peer pressure exerts tremendous force at this point. We charismatics are often desperate to speak in tongues because, after all, "everyone is doing it." We don't want to be left out and seen as unspiritual. It is a basic characteristic of human nature to seek preeminence among one's peers, and some have later confessed that they actually lied concerning their experiences "in the Spirit" in the excitement of the moment.

The Holy Spirit didn't take too kindly to being lied to by Ananias and Sapphira (Acts 5:1-11). What makes us think He appreciates it today? "Pride goes before destruction, and a haughty spirit before stumbling" (Proverbs 16:18).

[2]   Dillow, Jody, *Speaking in Tongues* (Zondervan, Grand Rapids, MI, 1975), p. 173.

But sometimes, in those with occult backgrounds or mediumistic tendencies, these techniques can open them even further to severe demonic deception and oppression.[3] One of the ways occultic powers are transferred from a spiritist or witch to someone else is through the laying on of hands. Those who have occultic gifts of tongues or healing or prophecy can and do pass these on by laying their hands on people thereby transferring their occultic gifts to them.[4] Dr. Koch, in his book *Strife of Tongues,* made the interesting observation "that people who are mediumistically inclined respond more quickly to speaking in tongues than others."[5] It is a tragedy that these people who suddenly find they have supernatural powers assume they must be from God. But it is not necessarily the Holy Spirit who is giving their talents.

For instance, Hindus speak in tongues. Buddhist and Shintoist priests speak in tongues while in a trance.[6] Cultists who deny the deity of Jesus speak in tongues. Many possessed Bantu natives in the Transvaal, South Africa, speak in tongues.[7] Some who are mentally ill speak in tongues. I myself have seen the demon-possessed and the spiritist mediums speak in tongues.

How, therefore, do we dare assert that speaking in tongues is the exclusive manifestation of the power and presence of the Holy Spirit in a believer's life? It is one

---

[3] Unger, Merill F., *What Demons Can Do to Saints* (Moody Press, Chicago, IL, 1977), pp. 81-84.

[4] Koch, Kurt E., *Strife of Tongues* (Kregel Publications, Grand Rapids, MI, 1966), pp. 25-28.

[5] Koch, Kurt E., *Strife of Tongues,* p. 33, 34.

[6] Koch, Kurt E., *Strife of Tongues,* p. 31.

[7] Koch, Kurt E., *Strife of Tongues,* p. 31.

of the most easily counterfeited of gifts and one of the most treacherous, for Satan has used it to take our focus off worshiping a mighty, sovereign Lord, puffing us up, rather, with a subtle, prideful preoccupation with our *gifting* instead of with our walk with God. Countless faithful lambs whose lives are characterized by the *fruit* of the Spirit and by faith and by power in their testimony for Messiah have never spoken in tongues. Many of these believers have been placed under awful burdens by those who demand for them what God may not have chosen to give them.

Whether it be the tongues of men or tongues of angels, the sign of tongues or the gift of tongues, there is no getting around the fact that the Holy Spirit distributes these just as He chooses, and according to His sovereign will.[8] (I Corinthians 12:28-30; 14:15-19; Hebrews 2:4; Romans 12:3-8)

Paul gives us this admonition in the context of this very subject:

> "Brethren, do not be children in your thinking; yet in evil be babes, but in your thinking be mature." (I Corinthians 14:20)

The Source of True Power

We cannot base our authority on our ecstatic feelings, and angelic visions, or point to miracles or aesthetic life-styles as proof of "good fruit" and power in our lives, as I have heard some do. These things mean nothing in and of themselves:

> "Let no one keep defrauding you of your prize by delighting in self-abasement and the worship of the angels, taking his stand on visions he has seen, inflated without cause by his fleshly mind, and not holding fast to the head . . . " (Colossians 2:18-19a)

These things may have an appearance of wisdom,

---

[8] Lindsey, Hal, *Satan is Alive and Well on Planet Earth* (Bantam, New York, 1972), pp. 137-149.

but are "of no value against fleshly indulgence" (Colossians 2:23).

In other words, it is not visions or disciplines or experiences which produce the power of God in our lives. Visions, even of Jesus, are easily counterfeited by Satan, as are tongues and prophecies and healings. There is no one experience, however ecstatic, that results in instant maturity.

Power in our lives comes by grace, from the Holy Spirit, as we *walk* with Him in yielded obedience. Power to walk by faith, power to resist temptation, power to minister and witness—this power is available to *every* believer, whether he has ever spoken in tongues or not.

The fruit of the Spirit (Galatians 5:22-23), maturity, is one of the true signs of the presence of the Spirit in a believer's life. Maturity comes only through abiding in Him—like the tree planted by the streams of living waters. "By this is My Father glorified, that you bear much *fruit,* and so prove to be My disciples" (John 15:8).

I know that those immersed in traditional charismatic teachings may disagree with what I have said here. But what if my observations are correct? Are you willing to stand before God for the error you have perpetuated? Because so many believers who do not speak in tongues have manifested such power of the Holy Spirit in their lives, I wonder whether we dare make a dogma of this subject.

Nowhere in the epistle to the Romans where Paul expounds upon every major doctrine, upon every major truth necessary to the believer's walk, does he mention tongues or any other miraculous sign or gift as the key to power in our lives. "Faith in God's promises alone is stressed. Would Paul have left out of this important treatise a truth that was the *key* to receiving power for serving and living for God?"[9]

Sincerity Plus Fifty Cents

It is not that God is giving the sincere believer a snake or a scorpion instead of a fish, but rather that we, in willful ignorance of the Word of God and of Satan's schemes, have grieved His Holy Spirit and allowed ourselves to be deceived.

The Lord has promised "what is good to those who ask Him" (Matthew 7:11), but John adds we have this confidence before Him if we ask *"according to His will"* (I John 5:14), and if we *"keep His commandments and do the things that are pleasing in His sight"* (I John 3:22).

Can it be His will for us to be undiscerning?

Can it be pleasing in His sight that we, like willful children, demand and seek to force His hand in the bestowing of gifts, allowing chaos and confusion to reign in our midst? Can it be pleasing in His sight that those whom *He* has not gifted with tongues are made to feel inferior and lacking in their faith and worthiness before Him? Can it be His will for faithful, committed believers to whom He has *not* given tongues to be thrown into an awful turmoil of their spirits because of this? I think not. In our zeal, we have turned a gift into a stumbling block.

Paul told us to "earnestly desire the greater gifts" (I Corinthians 12:31; 14:1). But this in no way implies that He plans to bestow one certain sign or *every* gift upon each believer. (I Corinthians 12:28-30; Hebrews 2:4). Hal Lindsey has pointed out that the command to desire the gifts is stated in the plural and addressed to the church, not individuals.

Let us ask with pure hearts, knowing that in His

---

[9]   Lindsey, Hal, *Satan is Alive and Well on Planet Earth*, p. 143.

sovereign love He will distribute His gifts and signs *just as He wills* (I Corinthians 12:11).

We do not need to plead or demand for gifts any more than we need demand His mercy. It is His very nature to grant them. His commandment to us is not to speak in tongues but rather that "we believe in the name of His Son Jesus Christ, and love one another" (I John 3:23). We are to seek *Him*. God is quite capable of seeing to it we manifest His gifts as a result.

Quenching the Spirit

Let us desire the gifts, but let us be discerning.

We have been told to test the spirits. The words of I John 4:1 are not phrased as a polite request to be employed if the mood strikes us: "Beloved, do not believe every spirit, but TEST the spirits to see whether they are from God; because many false prophets have gone out into the world"—producing *signs* and *wonders* and *miracles;* looking and acting and sounding on the surface like the genuine article.

Yet I see many of us persist in refusing to test these tongues, these prophecies, these healings and miracles, afraid, somehow, that it shows a lack of faith—that in our testing we will quench the Holy Spirit. But look at the Word of God:

> Do not quench the Spirit; do not despise prophetic utterances. But *examine* everything *carefully;* hold fast to that which is good. (I Thessalonians 5:19-21)

Concerning the Bereans, we are told these were "more noble-minded than those in Thessalonica, for they received the word with great eagerness, *examining the Scriptures daily,* to see whether these things were so" (Acts 17:11). They put the words of Paul himself to the test against the unchangeable testimony of the Word of God instead of merely relying on their *feelings* to verify the truth he brought them. The true prophets of God have never been afraid to make "careful search" (I Peter 1:10-11) concerning what the Spirit spoke to them.

It is not *testing* the Spirit that quenches Him, but rather it is sin, rebellion, disobedience and willful ignorance which grieve Him. The only one who is insecure about testing the gifts is the one who doesn't know the Scriptures, for they tell us such practice proves the genuine and pleases God.

Unless the church recognizes this and repents before the Lord, seeking to bring restoration and purity to the body which is now polluted by counterfeits and false doctrines, how will we survive these days? We will be rent apart by strife and factions. We will be as salt that has lost its taste, and how then will we be able to reach a world dying in the stranglehold of occult deception with the glorious truth of our victory in Christ?

As it is, occultists usually feel right at home in our meetings, for they see the whooping down of the Spirit, shaking hands "uncontrollably" in techniques that smack of aura manipulation, falling into trance-like states, and crying out "words of knowledge" just as the clairvoyants do in certain spiritualist centers. They see us *demanding* God's immediate performance as do white magicians who also use the name of God and Jesus and the Holy Spirit in their rituals. They see us literally barking like dogs "in the spirit".[10] They see us being bounced off the floor by an unseen force, even as I frequently saw happen to Pachita when she was possessed. They hear a deafening confusion of babbling tongues, each one screaming louder than the next, as though the Lord were deaf. They see us indiscriminately laying on hands for healing, even as they do, with no call whatever to confession and repentance of sin,

---

[10]   I heard this event proclaimed in one meeting as a marvelous example of the liberty and "freedom from inhibitions" that we have in the Spirit.

(which also thrives among us) (James 5:14-17).

How then can we call the occultist to repentance? How then can we presume to call him into a relationship with the Holy, Living God in whom there are no "shifting shadows" (James 1:17)? "God is not a God of confusion but of peace, as in all the churches of the saints" (I Corinthians 14:33).

It does not "inhibit the spirit" or "box God in" to establish order in our meetings. Or so Paul believed:

> If anyone thinks he is a prophet or spiritual, let him recognize that the things which I write to you are the Lord's commandment. But if anyone does not recognize this, he is not recognized. Therefore, my brethren, desire earnestly to prophesy, and do not forbid to speak in tongues. But let all things be done properly and in an orderly manner. (I Corinthians 14:37-40).

Why Study?

I am not suggesting we need live in perpetual paranoic dread of demons and counterfeits creeping in our midst. The church does not need an onslaught of witch hunters and self-appointed fruit-and-gift inspectors sweeping through our assemblies. Nor am I suggesting that every believer need focus his attention on becoming an expert on Satan and demons and the things of darkness. As believers our call is to focus on Jesus, to worship *Him,* to keep our eyes on *Him,* to come to know and love *and* experience Him above all else.

To that purpose God has called His children to study, to present themselves approved to God as workmen who need not be ashamed, "handling accurately the word of truth" (II Timothy 2:15). That takes some effort, and somehow many of us have come to believe that the systematic study of the Bible is "legalistic" and vaguely unspiritual. The Bible—the word of God—"is living and active and sharper than any two-edged sword, and piercing as far as the division of soul and spirit, of both joints and marrow, and able to judge the thoughts and intentions of the heart" (Hebrews 4:12).

It is the "sword of the Spirit" (Ephesians 6:17b) which is the one offensive weapon in the armor God has provided for us. It is the one weapon which can, when wielded by a believer controlled by the Spirit of the Lord, cause the greatest destruction to Satan's kingdom. This is why Satan will always seek to attack the Word and weaken the believer's grasp on that deadly sword. He will seek to disarm us, leaving us with no weapon to use against him, or to use in our defense. However strong a soldier's armor, without the sword the enemy will soon strike him down and destroy him.

Any attitude which lessens or undermines the authority of the Word must be suspect. It is that Word through which God has revealed what we *must* know about Him and our salvation. It is not meant to be an exhaustive revelation—but any other revelation which does not stand in harmony and agreement with the Word—however righteous it may feel or sound—is not from God. Yet I have heard brothers in our midst assert they have no need for systematic study, or even for devotional reading from the Word, for God always "speaks to them directly, telling them exactly what to do."

Jim Jones adopted that premise and because his followers did not compare his words to those of Holy Scripture, they were led into hideous destruction.

We should be cautious when anyone asks us to "just put your theology aside for a moment." It usually indicates that what follows is based on someone's experience taken over and above the context of the

Word. If it doesn't *fit into* proper theology, perhaps it has no business being there at all.

Knowledge and understanding of Scripture will not come through the odd and ancient process of "absorbtum mysterium." It comes as the result of hard work as well as by the quickening of the Holy Spirit. We neglect it at our peril.

17
Test The Spirits

We have been commanded to test the spirits. Very well. But just exactly how do we do that? How can we be certain a healing or a miracle is from God? How can we be sure our own gifts are from the Lord?

God has not offered us His supernatural gifts and power only to leave us permanently contorted by the terror that it may all be a demonic counterfeit. Many pastors have felt a reluctance to discuss counterfeits at all for fear of that very thing. As a result, many of us are left in ignorance of Satan's schemes and techniques and therefore vulnerable to them. It is the naive and the ignorant who are most easily taken in by the silken tongue of the con-man.

It is important for us to "pin the tail on the donkey" in these matters (though not necessarily in the sense Balam may have wanted to).

Spirit of Prophecy

There are several basic tests given by the Lord in His Word which help us distinguish the true prophets from the false ones. This task is not always a simple one, for a false prophet will rarely oblige us by admitting to it up front. Therefore, it is important to discern on the basis of *all* these tests, not just one or two. The tests covered herein can also be applied to signs and wonders.

In the Old Testament a prophet was "divinely inspired to *communicate God's will* to His people and to *disclose the future* to them."[1] [Italics mine.] The word prophet, *nabi,* means "a declarer, announcer, one who utters a communication announcing, pouring forth, the declarations of God."[2] They were the shepherds and watchmen of Israel who bore testimony to the one true God (Isaiah 45:6). Theirs was the responsibility of admonishing the people for their sins, calling them to repentance and righteous living, speaking not only of the divine judgment of sin, but of the love and compassion of the Lord upon those who turned from their evil ways to walk in faith before Him.

Their calling as prophets was not only to foretell the future as revealed to them by God, but to call the people into obedient relationship with Him (Deuteronomy 29:29).

Revelation 19:10 proclaims the ultimate purpose and goal of prophecy: "For the *testimony of Jesus* is the spirit of prophecy."

Which Jesus?

1. The first test of a prophet (or a healer) must be in the area of doctrine: *What does he believe about Jesus?* Does he cling to Jesus Christ of Nazareth as God the Son, second Person of the Trinity, God incarnate in human flesh; the God-Man who died upon the cross in our place for the forgiveness of our sins; the One born of a Virgin whose physical resurrection from the dead proclaimed His victory over sin, death and Satan? Does that person believe it is "by grace you

[1] Unger, Merrill F., *Unger's Bible Dictionary* (Moody Press, Chicago, IL 1961) pp. 890-893.

[2] Ibid

have been saved through faith; and that not of yourselves, it is the gift of God; not as a result of works, that no one should boast"? (Ephesians 2:8). Or have they, through subtle redefinition, come to accept "another Jesus," "another Spirit," "another gospel"?

This is what John means when he says "every spirit that confesses that Jesus Christ has come in the flesh is from God; and every spirit that does not confess Jesus is not from God; and this is the spirit of the antichrist . . ." (I John 4:2-3a).

So, the first question to be asked is "Which Jesus?" "Which gospel?" For if the answers to these two questions are not the right ones, then you automatically know "which spirit."

In Deuteronomy 13:1-5 the Lord states clearly that even if that prophet or dreamer of dreams works genuine miracles, if he in any way seeks to lead you into trusting in another god, you are not to listen to him, "for the Lord your God is testing you to find out if you love the Lord your God with all your heart and with all your soul."

Jesus said, "He who has my commandments, and keeps them, he it is who loves Me, and he who loves Me shall be loved by My Father, and I will love him and will disclose Myself to him" (John 14:21). It is not enough to mouth the words of our love for Jesus on the one hand while practicing those things which are contrary to His written Word on the other.

In Deuteronomy 18, the Lord warns us that the false prophet may even come using the name of God, saying "thus says the Lord"—as did every true prophet. Following is another acid test which precious few prophets of today would pass.

One Hundred Percent Accurate
2. *They must be one hundred percent accurate*

one hundred percent of the time. "And you may say in your heart, 'How shall we know the word which the Lord has not spoken?' When a prophet speaks in the name of the Lord, if the thing does not come about or come true, that is the thing which the Lord has not spoken. The prophet has spoken it presumptuously; you shall not be afraid of him" (Deuteronomy 18:21-22). The prophets of today, as perhaps you've noticed, have a tendency towards inaccuracy. Even Jean Dixon's failings are staggering. It is not enough to assure us you've just had an "off day," or "the vibrations weren't just right," or to assert you *were* correct in your prediction but the person whose vibrations you had read suddenly changed his mind.

It should be obvious to us that God knows well enough whether that would happen and could have said it right the first time. If the word had been from Him, it would have been *one hundred percent on target.* That criterion should apply even within charismatic meetings, but it seldom does. It is not enough to excuse these inaccuracies by saying "But what do you expect; I'm new at this, and any way, it must be from God. I feel it in my spirit." Our feelings are not the ultimate test.

Prophets in the Old Testament spoke forth the Word and will of God in inspired teaching in addition to giving prophetic words about the future. The gift of speaking forth God's Word to help strengthen and confirm the faith of the believer, to speak the secrets of the heart in order that the unbeliever may come to *know* God's love and personal concern for him is indeed operative today. Let each look to himself lest he degrade that calling by reducing it to the level of fortunetelling. If a person claims to predict the future in the name of the Lord, then that one is subject in *every* respect to what God said in Deuteronomy 18:20-22 and 13:1-5.

Abomination

3. *If a miracle or sign or prophecy or healing is performed by an occultist, or by means of occultic techniques, it is not from God.* It is counterfeit. For "what fellowship has light with darkness, or what harmony has Christ with Belial?" (2 Corinthians 2:14-15). None whatever.

God made his position on the occult remarkably clear in Deuteronomy 18:9-14 where he lists the full gamut of occult categories and flatly labels them *detestable* (the King James Version uses the word *abominable*). In case we missed it the first time around, He repeats it three times (verse 9 and twice in verse 12). It is not because these occultists were "stealing away business," but because God knows the demonic source behind these practices and does not want His people to be contaminated by them (Leviticus 19:31). Those who turn to mediums and to spiritists are spiritual harlots in the eyes of God (Leviticus 20:6), and are deserving of death accordingly (Exodus 22:18), for these things lure the people away from dependence on God, causing them to turn to demons instead in their seeking after hidden things which are forbidden (Deuteronomy 29:29).

It is fortunate that we no longer live in a theocracy such as was Israel, for our population today would be decimated. If we are walking in faith and dependence upon the Lord, our God, we do not need to know as much about our immediate future as some might suppose. It is enough that He holds our future in His hands, and that we can, therefore, dare to walk by faith.

And when they say to you, 'Consult the mediums and the wizards who whisper and mutter,' should not a people consult their God? Should they consult the dead on behalf of the living? To the law and to the testimony! If they do not speak according to this word, it is because they have no dawn (Isaiah 8:19-20) (see also Isaiah 45:11).

If any prophet who claimed to be speaking for the Lord was found to practice divination or sorcery or spiritism or any occult technique, he was immediately recognized as one whom God had not sent (Ezekiel 22:28; Jeremiah 14:14; 28:8-9; Micah 3:7). The true prophets had no need of these techniques, for God is fully able to speak His word to them through revelation and inspiration when He chooses. In *An Introduction to the Old Testament Prophets,* author Dr. Hobart Freeman says, "This is one of the greatest distinctions between the religion of Israel and heathen religions who sought to discover truth by means of divination and sorcery."[3]

God spoke through His prophets by inspiration and dreams and visions, not through occultic techniques. His dealings with occultists in the New Testament, such as the girl with the spirit of divination in Acts 16:18, and the magician and false prophet Bar-Jesus in Acts 13:6-11, clearly indicate He has not changed His mind on the subject. We "cannot drink the cup of the Lord and the cup of demons" (1 Corinthians 10:21).

But as Dr. Freeman also points out, false prophets receive dreams and visions as well and may not use actual techniques of divination, such as crystal balls or tarot cards or Ouija boards or astrology, or tea leaf reading, etc.

That is why *all* these tests must be applied.

No single test, in and of itself, is sufficient. A false

[3] Freeman, Hobart E., *An Introduction to the Old Testament Prophets* Moody Press, Chicago, IL 1968), p. 110.

prophet or wonder worker might pass one or two of these tests alone yet still be speaking lies and producing counterfeits.

Fruit of Life

4. *The test of the fruit of life must also be applied.* Most false prophets in the Old Testament were characterized by consistently unrepentant low moral standards and generally raunchy lives, however whitewashed they might have been on the surface for public viewing. A true prophet of the Lord should walk according to the light of His calling. We do see true prophets of the Lord, such as David, sinning grievously for a season. Murder and adultery are hardly trivial. But what made David a man after God's own heart was that he was honest to recognize his sin before God and repent. What often characterizes false prophets is a rebellious, unrepentant spirit. But not always.

Frequently their *lives*, their moral standards, are totally above reproach. The fruit of their lives could put many of us to shame. Matthew 7:15-23 is a key passage here. The Lord is warning us against the false prophets "who come to you in sheep's clothing, but inwardly are ravenous wolves" (verse 15). How will we spot them? "You will know them by their fruits" (verse 16). The Lord then goes to great lengths to explain the basics of spiritual agriculture, re-emphasizing that a good tree cannot produce bad fruit and vice versa. However, most people never read past the verse that again says "so then you will know them by their fruits" (verse 20).

Not everyone who says to Me, 'Lord, Lord,' will enter the kingdom of heaven; but he who does the will of My Father, who is in heaven. Many will say to Me on that day, 'Lord, Lord, did we not prophesy in Your name, and in Your name cast out demons, and in Your name perform many miracles?' And then I will declare to them, 'I never knew you; *depart from Me, you who practice lawlessness'* (verses 21-23).

It was not enough that these who used the name of the Lord prophesied or cast out demons or even performed many miracles. The fruit of their life, in and of itself, was worth nothing. Good works don't earn your way into heaven.

They said therefore to Him, 'What shall we do, that we may work the works of God?' Jesus answered and said to them, 'This is the work of God, that you believe in Him whom He has sent' (John 6:28-29) (see also I John 3:23).

It is the "fruit of doctrine" that gives eternal value to the "fruit of life." Without a personal relationship with Jesus as Lord and Savior, the fruit of life is ultimately meaningless.

Inner Witness[4]

5. *The final test is that of our subjective inner witness.* I have spoken a good deal about the desperate need within our body for building upon the solid objective base of Scripture, for it is through that clear, clean Word that God Himself reveals His Son—our Cornerstone. It is through the Word that He equips us. But ultimately we come before our God on a deeply intimate and personal level in which we feel His love and tender compassion for us; in which we experience the joy and deep serenity of His presence in our lives. The supreme goal of our existence is to love and know . . . experience . . . Him.

When we walk in fellowship with our Lord, as we come to know Him, His Holy Spirit bears witness within us concerning these things. But where we have grieved His Holy Spirit through sin and disobedience, this inner witness becomes warped and distorted and

[4]   Ibid

we no longer see or understand. Our inner witness may no longer be accurate.

The Lord said, "If any man is willing to do His will, he shall know of the teaching, whether it is of God, or whether I speak from Myself" (John 7:17). If we truly want to know the Truth and are willing to be obedient to it, God will make it evident within us.

Sadly, too many of us insist our inner witness is the first and most important criterion (But I myself once said ". . . How can you tell me the work at Pachita's is demonic! I have felt the presence of the evil beings, I have experienced the good; I can tell the difference. . .").

18
The Means Of Freedom

The five basic tests of the spirits will go a long way towards weeding out the counterfeit from the genuine. But the question still remains: How do you test the genuineness of your own gifting before the Lord? How do you shut the door to any occultic influence that may be operating in your life?

There are no special secret rituals involved in this, but it is nonetheless important to understand some basic principles of Scripture concerning these things.

It may be that some of you who are reading these words do not believe in Jesus as your Lord and Savior. Some of you may have read this far out of sheer curiosity; but some of you may have read this because you are seeking release from demonic bondage.

No Freedom Apart From Jesus
1. Understand then, before anything else, that apart from Jesus there is no hope for you. "There is salvation in no one else; for there is no other name under heaven that has been given among men, by which we must be saved" (Acts 4:12 KJV).

Unless you are prepared to commit your life, your body, mind and spirit, to His Lordship, you will never find the peace and freedom that you seek. "Come to Me, all who are weary and heavy laden, and I will give you rest" (Matthew 11:28), Jesus says to you. His yoke is easy. His load is light.

Satan will yoke you to his lies. He will lure you as an angel of light that he may ultimately burden you with terror and destruction. But the awesome witness of the Scriptures is that "The Son of God appeared for this purpose, that He might *destroy the work of the devil*" (I John 3:8).

It is He who has "disarmed the rulers and authorities," for "He made a public display of them, having triumphed over them through Him" (Colossians 2:15). It is Jesus who through death upon a cross rendered "*powerless* him who had the power of death, that is, the devil" (Hebrews 2:14). But "how shall we escape if we neglect so great a salvation?" (Hebrews 2:3). He has obtained the victory, but it is useless to the one who rejects Him. "Today if you hear His voice do not harden your hearts" (Hebrews 3:15).

For All Time

Those who stand in Jesus need never fear the loss of that salvation. "*All* that the Father gives Me shall come to Me; and the one who comes to Me I will certainly not cast out . . . . of *all* that He has given Me *I lose nothing,* but raise it up on the last day" (John 6:37, 39).

For Him to lose a single one of us who has come to Him in faith would make of Him a liar, for He has said *all* who come shall be raised up with Him. We cannot somehow undo what Christ has done at the cross. "For by one offering He has perfected *for all time* those who are sanctified" (Hebrews 10:14). "By this we have been sanctified through the offering of the body of Jesus Christ *once for all*" (Hebrews 10:10). The forgiveness He obtained for us is eternal. It cannot be taken back. To believe it can is to say that somehow the sacrifice that Jesus made on our behalf was not sufficient, that He was somehow lacking.

But Paul tells us that

> God, being rich in mercy, because of His great love with which He loved us, *even when we were dead in our transgressions*, made us alive together with Christ (by *grace* you have been saved), and *raised us* up with Him, and *seated us* with Him in the heavenly places, in Christ Jesus, in order that in the ages to come He might show the surpassing riches of His grace in kindness towards us in Christ Jesus (Ephesians 2:4-7). [Italics mine]

All of our sins were in the future when Christ died on the cross. He died not only for the sins we committed *before* accepting His forgiveness, but for all the sins we might commit afterwards as well. The only sin which He cannot forgive is that of going into eternity having rejected Him.

> I said therefore to you, that you shall die in your sins; for unless you believe that I am He, you shall die in your sins (John 8:24).

But "if any man is in Christ, he is a new creature" (II Corinthians 5:17a). Because He took our sins upon Himself and paid the penalty for them, God the Father is no longer hostile towards us; *all* our transgressions have been forgiven, for the decrees against us were *paid in full* at the cross (Colossians 2:13-14).

> I, even I, am the one who wipes out your transgressions for My own sake; and I will not remember your sins (Isaiah 43:25).

All who are in Him are *now* seated with Him (Ephesians 2:6) at the throne of God. Our *position* there is secure, for Jesus Himself said:

> My sheep hear My voice, and I know them, and they follow Me; and I give eternal life to them; and they shall *never* perish, and *no one* shall snatch them out of My hand. My

Father, who has given them to Me, is greater than all; and no one is able to snatch them out of the Father's hand (John 10:27-29).

Not even *we* can take ourselves out of the Father's hand once we are His.

Satan's Goal

Since, therefore, our souls are forever secure, what is it that Satan is seeking to steal away from us who are in Christ?

C. S. Lewis said it: "The next best thing to a damned soul is a sterile Christian."

Satan would rob us of our witness, making us into stumbling blocks to those who are perishing; he would rob us of our peace and of our joy; he would rob us of our freedom; he would rob us of our fellowship with God. This is why we are *constantly* exhorted to walk according to the light (I John 1:6-7); to be on the alert (I Peter 5:8); to "put on the full armor of God that (we) may be able to stand firm against the schemes of the devil" (Ephesians 6:11).

Blatant immorality, the deeds of the flesh in Galatians 5:19-21, pride and rebellion, participation in the things which God has called abomination, all give Satan the toe-hold he seeks in our lives in one way or another. Occult activities especially make us vulnerable to demonic oppression. This is why it is important to "shut the door" which we may have opened in our lives to his influence.

Writing a "Stop" Payment

2. Every sin connected with sorcery constitutes, in a very real sense, a pact with the devil.[1] It gives him the legal right to bind and oppress that person (Exodus 20:3-5), *regardless* of how that door was opened. Perhaps you were charmed by a medium or a healer as a child; perhaps you inherited the demonic burden

[1] Koch, Kurt E., *Occult Bondage and Deliverance* (Kegel Publications, 1968), p. 100.

through your family line, even as I did. It may be that someone with mediumistic gifts layed hands on you, thereby transferring his powers to you to some degree. Perhaps you only "played around" with a Ouija board, or with aura manipulation or with astrology. The fact that you may have only viewed these things as a joke doesn't make a bit of difference to Satan. Once you trespass into his territory you may well become fair game and the focus of demons.

Regardless of how it happened, there is only one way to shut the door: through coming to Jesus in confession and renunciation.

To confess our sins means simply to acknowledge them before God; that is, to agree with Him that what we have done was wrong and in violation of His will. It is important that this confession of one under occult oppression take place, if possible, in the presence of a mature believer, or a Christian counselor, for two reasons:

(a) *To bring into the light the secret, hidden things.* The occultists in Ephesus who turned to the Lord "kept coming, confessing and disclosing their practices" (Acts 19:18), renouncing the hidden things (II Corinthians 4:2). It is especially important that every known resentment and sin be confessed, not only those connected with occultism, so that any foothold Satan may seek to keep in our lives is removed. This confession cannot be forced from the person. If it is not voluntary—from the heart—it is worthless.[2]

(b) *To lift you up in prayer* as you legally revoke Satan's claim in your life. The devil will not be pleased and may, in some cases of severe oppression, put up a struggle before releasing his hold.

Spend some time before you pray considering the things you will want to confess. In some cases it may be helpful even to make a list of these things, asking God

[2] Koch, Kurt E., *Occult Bondage and Deliverance*, pp. 98-99.

to show you what it is you need to bring before Him.

Destroy Occult Objects

It is also *most* important that you collect every book or object related to occultism in your possession and destroy them. Don't just throw them in a garbage can where your neighbors can get at them. Make sure the objects are smashed, burned, or ripped beyond repair. These things often act as crystalization points for demons. Get rid of them (Acts 19:19).

Prayer of Renunciation

The following prayer of confession and renunciation can be used, but the words themselves are not somehow sacred. It is the intent and attitude of the heart which matters before God.

> Almighty God, in the Name of your Son Jesus, I renounce all the works of the devil.
> I confess and renounce all my occultic practices and sins as abomination before You. (list them here)
> I renounce any occult influences from my forefathers and I ask, Lord God, that You now break any hold Satan may have had in my life because of them.
> I pray that any evil power or ability I may possess, or which has oppressed or possessed me, be completely destroyed and removed from me, for I want no gift that isn't Yours.
> I commit myself, my body, my mind, my personality, my emotions, my whole being, to the Lord Jesus Christ to be my Savior and my Lord.

Just as our salvation is by grace, through faith, "and that not of yourselves; it is the gift of God; not as a result of works . . . " (Ephesians 2:8) so it is with our deliverance from demonic bondage. It is not based on our performance or merit. It is not dependent on our feelings. Regardless of your emotional state at this point, if you have come before God with an open heart in this confession, you have the assurance of the Word of God that "He is faithful and righteous to forgive us our sins and to cleanse us from all unrighteousness" (I John 1:9). The door has now been closed. Don't let Satan steal away your assurance, although you can be certain he will try. We will speak shortly of the weapons God has made available to us for that battle.

Test Your Gifts

For those of you seeking to test your gifts before the Lord, much the same form can be used. Spend time in prayer and confession and worship. Ask Him to grant you discernment in this matter. Then simply offer back to Him any supernatural gift or healing you may have received:

> Father, I give back to you this gift of tongues, or healing, or miracles, or prophecy . . . If it is indeed from You, then bless it and cause it to grow, that Your body may be blessed and edified through it.

> But if I have somehow been deceived in this, I ask that You remove it from Me. I renounce and reject this gift if it is not from You.

> Abba, give me a hunger for your Word; cause me to grow in the knowledge of Your love and grace. Cause me to seek You, sovereign God, above all else. I ask these things in the Name of Your Son, my Lord and Savior Jesus Christ, knowing that my request is pleasing in Your sight. Amen.

Having tested your healing or your gift against the Word of God, in obedience to His command; having through confession and renunciation shut the door to occult bondage, if indeed this was applicable to your life; having placed yourself and your gift in the capable hands of our God, walk therefore in the glory of His might and in joyful confidence of His protection!

> Is anyone among you suffering? Let him pray. Is anyone cheerful? Let him sing praises. Is anyone among you sick? Let him call for the *elders* of the church, and let them pray over him, anointing him with oil in the name of the Lord; and the prayer offered in faith will restore the one who is

sick, and the Lord will raise him up, and if he has committed sins, they will be forgiven him. *Therefore, confess your sins to one another,* and pray for one another so that you may be healed. The effective prayer of a righteous man can accomplish much. (James 5:14-16)

God *wants* us to ask wonderful things from Him. It is His delight to give every good and perfect gift to His children, for He loves us. He wants us to ask in confidence—not in fear of demons or counterfeits, but neither in undiscerning ignorance, which is a far cry from childlike faith.

Come before the Lord. Purify yourself before Him; "like the Holy One who called you, be holy yourselves in all your behavior; because it is written 'You shall be Holy, for I am Holy" ' (I Peter 1:15-16). It is holiness and right standing before our God which brings the true power of the Holy Spirit in our lives.

Would that we, like Paul, could rejoice in that His *grace* is sufficient for us, "for power is perfected in weakness" (II Corinthians 12:9).

Would that we, like Paul, could "count all things to be loss in view of the surpassing value of knowing Christ Jesus my Lord" (Philippians 3:8).

The Blood of the Lamb
3.   The end days are upon us. False Christs and false prophets and false miracles will continue to increase as the second coming of the Messiah draws nearer.

But however subtle the deceit, however furious the warfare, the believer who clings in obedience and in faith to the Messiah need NEVER retreat in fear at the onslaught of the demons or their counterfeits. The one who in obedience to God's command puts the spirits to the test cannot long be deceived.

It is not enough, though, not to be deceived. We must become active warriors in these evil days, knowing that *in Him* we are *more* than conquerors (Romans

8:37). It is the demons who flee in terror before the one who understands the victory and the power in the shed blood of the lamb. It is that blood which has shattered Satan's grasp upon us.

> And I heard a loud voice in heaven, saying, "Now the salvation, and the power, and the kingdom of our God and the authority of His Christ have come, for the accuser of our brethren has been thrown down, who accuses them before our God day and night. And they overcame him because of the blood of the Lamb and because of the word of their testimony, and they did not love their life even to death." (Revelation 12:10-11)

This is the greatest weapon God has given to His people: the protection of the blood of the Lamb, that blood which has cleansed us from all sin. Because you are in Him, you have the authority to plead that covering as protection in the battle against the devil.

Commanding Satan

Because of that shed blood, we can dare come against the devil, commanding him to flee before the name of Jesus. "I command you in the name of Jesus Christ to come out of her!" Paul ordered the spirit of divination who possessed the slave girl. Luke 10:17 records the joy of seventy disciples who exulted in the fact that "even the demons are subject to us in Your Name!"

We can dare command the devil *only* because of our position in Christ. We have no power in and of ourselves, so beware of getting haughty with the demons, ordering them into the pit—for even Michael the archangel, "when he disputed with the devil and argued about the body of Moses did not dare pronounce against him a railing judgment, but said, 'The Lord rebuke you.' " (Jude 9).

Some men "revile the things which they do not understand" (Jude 10).

But in the victory of Christ, as we stand under the authority and protection of His blood, as we are filled, that is, controlled by His Holy Spirit, we can command:

> Satan, in the Name of Jesus Christ I bind you and rebuke you. I command you to depart and go where Jesus sends you.

> I remind you I am a child of the Living God; you have no authority over me.

Then ask the Lord's covering:

> Father, I plead the covering and protection of Your blood. Fill me and shield me about with Your Holy Spirit.

These words are not a magic formula to be churned out as an automatic mantra. Nor are they a prayer to Satan. They are, rather, a word of command issued by an embattled child who understands the fierceness of spiritual warfare and the authority granted him by our victorious General.

Those who have come out of occultic backgrounds may find themselves resorting to this command many, many times throughout the day, as I myself did. Satan does not let go easily. He knows he has lost the battle for the soul, but will nonetheless rage against him. Do not be afraid. That is perhaps the greatest weapon Satan can throw at a believer. But God has said "His perfect love casts out all fear." When you feel Satan come against you, know you have the authority—the command—to resist him. He *will* flee from you (James 4:7).

God's Armor

4. Make use of the *full* armor of God. No warrior goes into battle with only the parts of his equipment that happen to appeal to him.

Because our struggle is not only against flesh and blood, but against the world forces of this darkness, against the spiritual forces of wickedness in heavenly places, *therefore* take up the full armor of God. Unless we are girded with the belt of His Truth, our armor will not hold together; unless we have put on the breastplate of righteousness of Christ, our hearts can be pierced through with pride and self-righteousness; unless our feet have the sturdy cleated shoes of the gospel of peace, we can be thrown off balance by the first wind of doctrine that hits us; unless we take up the shield of faith, Satan's flaming missiles of doubt and temptation will lodge deep in our flesh and burn us; the helmet of our salvation guards our minds; the sword of the Spirit, which is the living Word of God, we alternately use to defend ourselves and thrust forward "piercing as far as the division of soul and spirit" (Hebrews 4:12).

In that sword we find the words of victory over fear. Write out those passages which speak to you and commit them to your heart. Use them against Satan when he seeks to smother you with fear. Psalm 91, 27, 3, 4; Romans 8; John 6; Deuteronomy 31:6-8; I John 4:18; I John 4:4 and 3:8; Colossians 2:15; Revelation 12:11ff; Isaiah 41:9b-10. The Bible is filled with dozens of these words of comfort and assurance.

How is this armor appropriated? How do we put on what God has said we need to stand firm against the schemes of the devil? It is upon our knees in prayer that this is done (Ephesians 6:18).

Never underestimate the power of prayer and worship in the battle against Satan! The Lord abides in the praises of His people. It is as we praise and worship the Living God that the darkness cringes back, for it cannot stand the presence of the Light.

More Than Conquerors

Ours need never be the pitiful tragedy of *The Exor-*

cist, or of the Luntzes in *Amityville Horror I and II,* or of the Warrens of *The Demonologist.* The "solutions" they offer those enslaved by the demonic terrors are heartbreaking and terrifying in their emptiness, for they offer what amounts to idol worship, using Christian symbols and rituals as superstitious fetishes, taking the name of the Lord in vain. For all the trappings of religious fervor, they give no indication that they acknowledge Jesus as their personal Lord and Savior. More than once their experiences in "liberation" of the demonically oppressed have resulted as that of the seven sons of Sceva. These Jewish exorcists saw the power in the name of Jesus when wielded by Spirit-controlled believers and simply added it to their own repertoire. "Jesus, I know," the demon they then sought to cast out observed, "and Paul I have heard of, but who are you?" and proceeded to beat them, wounding them severely (Acts 19:13-16).

Remember there is a beautiful side of evil—deceptive, subtle, adorned with all manner of spiritual refinements, but no less from the pit of hell than that which is blatantly demonic.

But to us who have believed it is said: "You are from God, little children, and have overcome them; because greater is He who is in you than he who is in the world" (I John 4:4).

> And this I pray, that your love may abound still more and more in real knowledge and all discernment, so that you may approve the things that are excellent, in order to be sincere and blameless until the day of Christ; having been filled with the fruit of righteousness which comes through Jesus Christ, to the glory and praise of God. (Philippians 1:9-11)

May He grant us the grace and wisdom in these last days to walk as children of the Light.

"For such men are false apostles, deceitful workers, disguising themselves as apostles of Christ. And no wonder, for even Satan disguises himself as an angel of light. Therefore, it is not surprising if his servants also disguise themselves as servants of righteousness; whose end shall be according to their deeds."

II Corinthians 11:13-15 (NASB)

"For they are the spirits of devils, working miracles, which go forth unto the kings of the earth and of the whole world . . ."

Revelation 16:14 (KJV)

"For false Christs and false prophets will arise and will show great signs and wonders, so as to mislead, if possible, even the elect."

Matthew 24:24 (NASB)

"Many will say to Me on that day, 'Lord, Lord, did we not prophesy in Your name, and in Your name cast out demons, and in Your name perform many miracles?' And then I will declare to them, 'I never knew you; *Depart from Me, you who practice lawlessness.*' "

Matthew 7:22-23 (NASB)

RECOMMENDED READING LIST

Barnhouse, Donald Grey; *The Invisible War* (Grand Rapids, Michigan: Zondervan Publishing House, 1965

Bjornstad, James; *Jeane Dixon/Edgar Cayce, 20th Century Prophecy* (Minneapolis, Minnesota: Dimension Books, 1969)

Bjornstad, James, and Johnsn, Shildes; *Stars, Signs and Salvation in the Age of Aquarius* (Minneapolis, Minnesota: Dimension Books, 1971)

Bruce, F.F.; *The New Testament Documents: Are They Reliable?* (Downers Grove, Illinois: InterVarsity Press, 1943)

Chafer, Lewis Sperry; *Satan His Motive and Methods* (Grand Rapids, Michigan: Zondervan Publishing House, 1919)

Dickason, C. Fred; *Angels Elect and Evil* (Chicago, Illinois: Moody Press, 1975)

Freeman, Hobart E.; *An Introduction to the Old Testament Prophets* (Chicago, Illinois, Moody Press, 1968)

Gasson, Raphael; *The Challenging Counterfeit* (New Jersey: Logos International, 1966)

Gruse, Edmond C.; *Cults and the Occult in the Age of Aquarius* (Nutley, New Jersey: Presbyterian and Reformed Publishing Co., 1974)

Guinness, Os; *The Dust of Death* (Downers Grove, Illinois: InterVarsity Press, 1973)

Hunt, Dave; *The Cult Explosion* (Eugene, Oregon: Harvest House Publishers, 1962)

Koch, Kurt; *Between Christ and Satan* (Grand Rapids, Michigan: Kregel Publications, 1962)

Koch, Kurt; *Christian Counselling and Occultism* (Grand Rapids, Michigan: Kregel Publications, 1972)

Koch, Kurt; *Demonology Past and Present* (Grand Rapids, Michigan: Kregel Publications, 1973)

Koch, Kurt; *Occult Bondage and Deliverance* (Grand Rapids, Michigan: Kregel Publications, 1978)

Koch, Kurt; *Satan's Devices* (Grand Rapids, Michigan: Kregel Publications, 1978)

Koch, Kurt; *The Devil's Alphabet* (Grand Rapids, Michigan: Kregel Publications, 1969)

Koch, Kurt; *The Strife of Tongues* (Grand Rapids, Michigan: Kregel Publications, 1969)

Lindsey, Hal; *Satan is Alive and Well on Planet Earth* (Grand Rapids, Michigan: The Zondervan Corporation, 1972)

Little, Paul E.; *Know What You Believe* (Downers Grove, Illinois: InterVarsity Press)

Little, Paul E.: *Know Why You Believe* (Downers Grove, Illinois: InterVarsity Press, 1968)

Martin, Walter; *Cults Reference Bible* (Santa Ana, California: Vision House, 1981)

Martin, Walter; *The Kingdom of the Cults* (Minneapolis, Minnesota: Bethany Fellowship, Inc. Publisher, 1965)

Martin, Walter; *The Riddle of Reincarnation* (Santa Ana, California: Vision House, 1977)

Montgomery, John Warwick; *Principalities and Powers* (Minneapolis, Minnesota: Bethany Fellowship, 1973)

Peterson, William J.; *Those Curious New Cults* (New Canaan, Connecticut: Keats Publishing, Inc., 1973)

Sanders, Oswald J.; *The Holy Spirit and His Gifts* (Grand Rapids, Michigan: Zondervan Publishing House, 1940)

Schaeffer, Francis A.; *True Spirituality* (Wheaton, Illinois: Tyndale House Publisher, 1971)

Stott, John R.W.; *Basic Christianity* (Grand Rapids, Michigan: William B. Eerdman's Publishing Company, 1958)

Stott, John R.W.; *Baptism and Fullness* (Downers Grove, Illinois: InterVarsity Press, 1964)

Swihart, Phillip J.; *Reincarnation, Edgar Cayce and the Bible* (Downers Grove, Illinois, InterVarsity Press, 1975)

Thomas, W.H. Grifith; *How We Got Our Bible and Why We Believe it is God's Word* (Chicago, Illinois: Moody Press, 1926)

Timmons, Tim; *Chains of the Spirit* (Washington, D.C.: Cannon Press, 1960)

Trumbull, Charles G.; *Victory in Christ* (Fort Washington, Pennsylvania: Christian Literature Crusade, 1959)

Unger, Merrill F.; *Beyond the Crystal Ball* (Chicago, Illinois: Moody Press, 1973)

Unger, Merrill F.; *Biblical Demonology* (Wheaton, Illinois: Scripture Press, 1952)

Unger, Merrill F.; *Demons in the World Today* (Wheaton, Illinois: Tyndale House Publishers, 1971)

Unger, Merrill F.; *What Demons Can Do To Saints* (Chicago, Illinois: Moody Press, 1977)

Wilson, Clifford, and Weldon, John; *Close Encounters* (San Diego, California: Master Books, 1978)

Wilson, Clifford, and Weldon, John: *Occult Shock and Psychic Forces* (San Diego, California· Master Books, 1980)

Weldon, John, and Levitt, Zola; *Psychic Healing—An Expose of an Occult Phenomenon* (Chicago, Illinois: Moody Press, 1982)